MW00616328

CHOOSING NEW WAYS FORWARD

Book 1:

Shifting Our Relationship with Trauma

Choosing New Ways Forward

Book 1:
Shifting Our Relationship with Trauma

Elizabeth Jo

HenschelHAUS Publishing, Inc.
Milwaukee, Wisconsin

Copyright © 2021 by Elizabeth Jo, LLC

All rights reserved.

This book developed from a lifetime of opportunities, observations, and conversations. It is meant to inspire and is not meant to direct, define, prescribe or diagnose.

Published by HenschelHAUS Publishing, Inc.

Milwaukee, Wisconsin

www.henschelHausbooks.com

ISBN: 978159598-880-5

E-ISBN: 978159598-868-3

LCCN: 2021945376

Printed in the United States of America

Gathering our threads
Summoning our grit
Being brave enough
To choose
Forward in connection
Presence with relief
Nourishing
Coming true
With the treasures of our love

TABLE OF CONTENTS

Author's Note 1

Preface 3

Identifying the Gap 9

Experiencing 13

When Trauma Came to My Table 19

Trauma Fills a Space 23

Life with Trauma 31

What Trauma Does Next 39

Living with Trauma as the Main Character 53

Trauma as the Director 65

Side by Side, Living with Truth 75

Finding My Rock 85

Forming a Bond and Building a Relationship 99

A New Spectrum 107

Traveling with Threat 109

Reading the Tread of Threat in Trauma's Footprints ... 127

Finding a Way to Choosing 145

First with Ourselves 159

Glossary of Concepts 169

Further Reading 175

About the Author 177

AUTHOR'S NOTE

Over many years of curious exploration and dynamic conversation, a new understanding has emerged that has given me a way of expressing the insights and possibilities in this book. I am exceedingly grateful for the opportunity to participate in and share some of these concepts and ideas.

As this conversation includes evermore voices, bringing new insights and possibilities forward, it will be helpful to have a common vocabulary. This first book focuses on the practices and reverberations of trauma, threat and Against in our experience.

In these pages, I explore trauma as a relationship that we have developed as we struggle to survive, a dynamic that has replaced our relationship with ourselves and each other. This trauma is a name that we give to the set of symptoms that we live with when we experience threat.

When we feel that our wellbeing is at risk, we recognize threat to our survival. This threat is not, however, only present from without. As we feel the immediacy of threat, we generate threat in response and continue a cycle that saturates our lives.

While threat and the resulting trauma are perpetuated, we act Against what we believe is generating these events. This stance Against is a key component as we engage with ourselves and each other. For example, it's interesting to note that while I don't need to capitalize "threat" or "trauma," which stand out in our minds and signal our attention, we are so conditioned to be Against that the meaning is missed if I simply write "against."

In addition to these key concepts, I have included a full glossary in the back of this book. The words that are included, while they may seem familiar, are described to clarify and illuminate this discussion.

Elizabeth

PREFACE

As we interact with ourselves, each other, and situations, we have learned to bring threat to our experience and we often act Against. This brings trauma to the forefront of our lives. As we build our lives around trauma, we often live in a state of being overwhelmed. We are overwhelmed as individuals and as

> *We have learned to pull in, narrowing our field of consideration and possibility.*

a whole. To cope, we have learned to pull in, narrowing our field of consideration and possibility; our experiences necessarily include elements of fear as we exist in this limited, trauma-based environment.

Through open and intimate conversations with ourselves and each other, we can begin to expand our understanding and broaden our scope. We can begin seeing further and actually hearing ourselves and each other. With conversation, our curiosity and creativity can come forward and develop in new ways. We can begin making choices where we have been reacting. We can begin inventing with broader

> *With conversation, our curiosity and creativity can come forward and develop in new ways.*

perspective. With clarity born of inner knowing, we can leave the practice of life-as-survival to our history.

We have been backing onto the edge of a steep cliff. Yet, as life began dramatically shifting in the spring of 2020, we have seen amazing changes. Individuals are gradually starting to build new lives that are truly gratifying. At the same time, people are dying tragic and traumatic deaths often filled with the very essence of humanity's struggle.

Our Earth is changing too, moving in ways that alter how life is understood and experienced. New weather patterns are developing; fires, droughts, floods, and melting glaciers are changing the landscape of our planet.

Many of us have learned to fear change; we often become overwhelmed and frequently shut down. How can we open to new experiences without feeling overwhelmed and threatened? When even our reactions to change seem traumatizing, how can we find a way forward? What will help us feel secure when threat plays this major role?

I will talk about personal trauma in order to shed light on these intricate ways that threat moves through our lives. While we all feel threatened in differing and personal ways, we move together in our response. Individually and as a group, we tend to stand Against what feels threatening. The resulting trauma permeates our experiences.

When we threaten ourselves, we cannot develop non-threatening resources for living with one another. I will discuss these experiences in order to provide clarity about how we can move in new ways, both individually and together. I will describe how we inflict threat, ensuring deeper trauma and how we can find alternatives as we develop new relationships with ourselves.

> *Individually and as a group, we tend to stand Against what feels threatening.*

This book is an invitation, an opportunity to talk about some of the ways that we live with ourselves and with each other. If we choose to expand our personal worlds—as we learn to understand, care for and enjoy who we are individually—new ways of moving together will naturally develop. We can become curious and inviting in places where trauma has become the determining factor.

This book is also a conversation, moments for experiencing, observing, discussing, discerning, and clarifying.

> *As we learn to understand, care for and enjoy who we are individually— new ways of moving together will naturally develop.*

I am extending an invitation to move together in exploration, bringing curiosity to our lives and interactions.

Although not "easy," we can embark together. We can discover possibilities for ourselves as individuals, for who we are as humanity, and for our world.

This is a conversation that began decades ago. Taking a new direction, I am now inviting you to join the conversation.

I am grateful for the countless conversations and opportunities to explore that have come before. I have the benefit of incredible counsel and truly open and inspiring love as I explore and consider this unfolding life.

With the forming of this book, Lucinda Hart, Sara Sage, and Brenda Statzer have offered valuable perspective and support. Linda Jo Devlaeminck, Ewa Kaminski, and Jacque Nelson have given countless hours and insights, listening to and developing this unfolding tale with me. Susan Yerigan has also brought her support and inspiration to this project as it has developed, even before I fully understood the direction it would take.

Michael Wiescher's writings on history and the history of science have given me both broad and intimate perspectives through his careful research into the human story and its progression. Of course, I cannot fully express my gratitude for the support and care that my son and his father have brought to my life and work.

I am honored to bring this collaboration to written form with the expert guidance of Kira Henschel. Beyond these pages, Eric Daft and Tina Nagel have brought so much to this growing conversation.

Thank you all for being part of my life and my passions.

IDENTIFYING THE GAP

In this time of virtual meetings, I'm excited for this chance to come together.

I've spent my life observing and enjoying our world. I've been curious and I've also been confused and angry about the trauma we experience. It seems that the overwhelming threat that we struggle with is consuming more and more of our time and attention. I am aware of the distance we have created between joy and trauma. I am curious about what we can create from this gap when we recognize other options.

I am offering this book because I believe there is an amazing possibility in shared conversation and I am inviting you to step into the field with me. I believe there is a field where we can meet and find comfort in gathering while we lean into the truth of trauma's impact, in our individual lives and in humanity as a whole.

This is an opportunity to recognize trauma in its facets and forms...the ones I know of and the ones that you have experienced. I'm also here to consider our intimate lives and our shared experiences, the life that we each are and the life that we are sharing. And I'm here to talk about threat and how we move with it, how it influences the choices we make on a personal level and within our shared environments and experiences.

The questions I am asking in these pages are the questions I have wondered about—questions that I have found, that have opened new insights and realizations for me. I am bringing these questions hoping that they might spark your curiosity as well, encouraging your voice in the creation of these pages. And also beyond these pages, as you expand your personal conversation and share your insights, opening new opportunities as you and we move forward.

You may find needs and desires beyond these pages, even beyond your current experiences. I hope you pursue these as they arise. This is the stuff of possibility.

I also urge you to care for yourself well. Becoming overwhelmed will not offer truly new experiences. New possibility is birthed from new understanding. Perhaps together, we will create a way forward that nourishes us in our individuality and as humanity.

Experiencing

I recognize that we often move through our lives observing and considering. Although we may leave space for experiencing, we often have particular times devoted to these experiences. For example, we may experience nature in a beautiful sunset while bringing more focus than experience to our daily living. These moments of experiencing may be even more distant from the time we spend contemplating, evaluating and reading. Further, we may consider reading an experience but not an interaction.

I hope that we can set our sense of order aside while we're together with these pages. Although this obviously isn't necessary, doing so will offer new opportunities. Participating in this conversation may open new insights and ways forward that we hadn't considered or, possibly, even imagined.

As we begin, please choose a sweater or jacket if you'd like—and there are mugs for water, coffee, tea, cider. Please pour yourself a cup and let's make our way to the fire out in the field. The grasses are crunchy this time of year, the frogs still gracefully cheering on the night.

I chose these chairs so that we can easily move and adjust our comfort levels, moving with the fire's warming currents as the winds shift through the evening sky. For me, there's a special feeling that I find when perching on a large rock; a few are there, in the in-between. Let's move things around a bit to make room for the chairs that you have. There is enough space for all of us.

I think the truth about our intentions shifts with us as we move about, grow and change. So, it's important to me that I say what I'm here to offer, right from the start, here in the beginning.

I am here to have a conversation with you. I'm here to share my ideas and to hear what you'd like to bring.

As we join the circle, I invite you to take a few long deep breaths. If you're like me and have taken one rather shallow breath, let's go ahead and reach for a couple more. Now let's rummage through that chest of gold within ourselves that we always have near and let's choose something dear.

Even if you don't believe you have treasures, think of something that you have a smile for, that gives you comfort, shares a warm moment. There's a place at the end of this chapter to write about, perhaps draw an image of your treasure. A place to say, I treasure this as part of my life.

Even as we hold our treasure in one hand, our other hand is often holding trauma. Unlike our treasures, trauma isn't personal and it isn't warm. And although we actually can hold our treasures in one hand while trauma fills the other hand, we rarely do. We often keep our treasures locked away for safe keeping.

> *Unlike our treasures, trauma isn't personal and it isn't warm.*

The trauma we are holding is actually a concept, an encapsulating word that gives us "safe distance" from our intimate feelings and circumstances. Doing its job well, trauma re-defines our lives.

> *Trauma is actually a concept, an encapsulating word that gives us "safe distance" from our intimate feelings and circumstances. Doing its job well, trauma re-defines our lives.*

Growing from our experiences with threat, trauma introduces blame, shame, helplessness and so much more. Trauma isolates us from affirming nourishment—sending true care to a small hidden space. Uncomfortable and difficult feelings are also hidden away in this confining closet. Once there, trauma doesn't ignore these feelings even though they are separated from us.

As we experience our lives, trauma feeds us these feelings through its filter, altering our perceptions. Soon, our experiences are occurring within relationships that have a basis in trauma. Trauma is experienced again and again as we live lives permeated by threat and move Against ourselves and each other in defense. The threat we perceive becomes the threat that we are involved with.

> *Our experiences are occurring within relationships that have a basis in trauma.*

In this way, our personal trauma infiltrates our moments and sets the rhythm and tone of our lives. These experiences bring fear and threat to replace our guidance systems; threat becomes the director as it shapes the voice of our feelings, convincing us that its voice is actually our own.

We have a much different experience with our treasures. Our treasures are truly our own. Maybe that's why we keep them in this chest, a place where they are hidden. A place that feels distant and safe from threat.

Yet, let's bring our treasures with us. Let's bring them out, seeing what our treasures look like in shared company. While we're using our own voices, sharing our treasures, sharing who we are in this conversation, trauma has no way to be. Threat has nothing to hold onto. We can share our treasures here without threat or fear of threat.

I treasure this as part of my life:

WHEN TRAUMA CAME TO MY TABLE

To understand clearly this discussion about trauma and how it moves to alter our experiences of ourselves and each other, I'll begin with the moment when my trauma came between me and my life. This will give us a starting place and some experience to work with as we consider the effect of threat as it moves in our individual lives and modifies our humanity.

I was having an amazing day. Just five years old, I felt very big when I was given a stool to stand on and taught how to iron.

> The effect of threat moves in our individual lives and modifies our humanity.

See, ironing was a big deal for me. My mother would iron while the little ones were asleep. The house was quiet, lunch had been eaten and there was about an hour when things seemed to relax. Mother would hum as she ironed and I'd take my position under the ironing board, feeling the warm steam drift to me in a wonderful scent of starch and hot cotton. As freshly pressed fabric inched its way down, I had a magical tent behind a fabulous misting waterfall.

And on one of these lovely days, she brought in a stool and said I could try; I just had to be careful not to scorch the sheet. It was a big white sheet and I did really well. I was amazed how the wrinkles disappeared. My arm was tired but the big iron didn't seem too heavy at all!

When I was done, Mother finished pressing the sheet and then folded it beautifully. I put it on the green card table with the freshly folded pillow cases and towels, on this that she called, "linens day."

That night after supper, sheet in hand, Daddy took me for a ride, a treat, just Daddy and "his girl."

I think we went to the edge of town where there were a lot of trees. There were fewer streetlights back then and it had become dark on this warm autumn night without a moon. A lot of men came and even though Halloween was over, they were wearing their sheets. As he put the sheet over his head, Daddy said that I couldn't talk. Then we went into the crowd. I couldn't see much.

Everything was very angry. There was a biting smell in my throat that also clenched on my skin, sounds swirling as I bit my lips. Angry swam around, rubbing the water in my eyes. And then I saw.

Suddenly, on the other side of the small fire, people in sheets came with a man and then he was hanging from a branch of the big old tree. I didn't know where his babies were, but he called for the Lord to protect his babies. Not thinking, I pushed past elbows and knees until they were behind me. I could see his face and he was seeing my eyes. I wonder if our eyes were the only ones there that night without a sheet to peer through. Then he was quiet. Then he stopped moving.

I stopped hearing the men in their sheets. All I could hear was the hush, the hush of the night, of the trees standing vigil all around me, the man's rope creaking on tree bark, a hush where all of the noise from those white sheets had been laughing and congratulating themselves about something.

I stopped smelling the anger. The fear didn't rub across me anymore. All I could feel, all I could taste or see was the world getting smaller. I thought, "The sun won't be able to get here. Not anymore."

There I was, a five-year-old child with long blond braids and a blue paisley dress under her playing-outside coat, standing on the grass touching my throat and, finding only my neck, remembering to breathe.

The only thing my father said as we went to the car was, "Oh, for Christ's sake," when he realized I'd wet my pants. He opened the back door, waiving me to the other side where he couldn't smell me and throwing his sheet in next to me.

I pressed into the door and looked over at Daddy as the headlights of a passing car made the orange of his cigarette less bright. He looked the same. I could tell that I looked different and for the first time, the cigarette smoke made me feel nauseous. I suddenly felt frantic, riding there in the back seat.

You see, a new companion had joined me, someone who hadn't even been properly introduced but who would eat at my table with me for a very long time. Trauma had arrived and as it came to sit with me in the back seat, my relationship with the bright light of possibility was sent to the closet so that there would be plenty of room for this new relationship.

Trauma Fills a Space

As we carefully consider trauma, coming to realize how it moves in and impacts our lives, let's recall that trauma is a name that we give to the set of symptoms that we live with when we experience threat.

What overwhelms us—what makes our experiences grow smaller, tightening so that we no longer move freely on our own behalf—are experiences that feel threatening. These experiences alert us. We put our treasures in a chest for safe keeping and the threatening experience becomes traumatizing.

Yet, when we are moving along in ways that feel safe, easy, reasonable, and comfortable, we may feel overwhelmed and still not add to our trauma. Even in times of crisis, we are able to work through what is happening and decide. However, when our wellbeing becomes tangled up with our experiences,

> *And even in times of crisis, we are able to work through what is happening and decide. In these times, we are not overwhelmed.*

a crisis becomes a threat. We then begin sorting through our moments, trying to find safe passage. As we learn to survive, we may find a way to move with our treasures; we may come to forget that we have treasures.

> When our wellbeing becomes tangled up with our experiences, a crisis becomes a threat.

In our world, we have woven threat through the fabric of our humanity. As we feel overwhelmed in our lives—the experience of a crisis, or even hearing about a difficulty, often generates threat. Feeling this threat can signal insurmountable danger to our survival.

This is when we develop a personal knowing of recurrent trauma, a tangle that binds our legs and restricts the choices we see.

All of our interactions are now tied up with this trauma that has become an important character in our intimate knowing of life. Trauma is tangled around our interactions with the world and so we sort through what we see, always looking for a way through the threat.

By the time I was taken to the lynching, I had already experienced many opportunities to believe

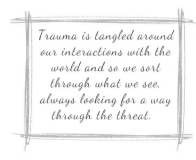

Trauma is tangled around our interactions with the world and so we sort through what we see, always looking for a way through the threat.

that I was a problem surrounded by problems. But, until that night, I didn't feel threatened. Until that night, I was busy simply noticing what people were doing, while living with what I treasured.

I was engaged with my treasures, living experiences that were about my thriving. I played "Kitchen" on the floor under the window, busily moving tiny, hand-sized bowls, pans and boxes around as I prepared wonderful meals for myself and my dolls; later, I cared for my brother and sister as we created a life of attention and wonder. I had my special red rocker, just big enough for me, where I went with my books, teaching myself to read by the time I had reached three years, entering worlds with people who were fun, curious, welcoming and encouraging.

Robert Louis Stevenson was there, smiling with me, gliding into the air on a swing:

> The world is so full of a number of things.
> I'm sure we should all be as happy as kings.

> —Robert Louis Stevenson
> "Happy Thought" in *A Child's Garden of Verses*

I also sat on the easement under the tree that the city had planted, reading in voices meant to engage my audience. I read to the worms and the grass on top, to the branches and the leaves as they grew, to the stray cat in the neighborhood who liked my fuzzy winter coat with the big red and pink flowers, so he'd snuggle into me and hum. I had had this experience, support, and practice. I knew who and where I was in this my deep inside, in this place with my treasures that had become my rock.

When threat moved in, trauma informed me that my known life had changed, that the sun's warmth could not continue to reach through. Much to my surprise, there were so many more people "out there" just like my family. There were so many angry people that, even with my book friends, my tree friends, and my bird friends—even with my wind and my flower friends—there would never be enough room for me.

Yet, on that night—when I became convinced that humanity could become inhumane—threat's reach did not fully envelop me.

I had already learned how to put my feelings away and then get them back out later, in spaces where I could be together with my full self without feeling threatened. On that night, however, I did begin to consider that I might not ever find a truly safe home—a place where I could bring my treasured feelings, curiosities and ideas, my treasures that are me. I began to believe that a place where there would be enough, a place where I could feel and celebrate myself and my life, might not actually exist. This was the beginning of my relationship with trauma.

Trauma would become so pervasive that I wouldn't even realize when I was actually safe. Further, I would come to feel comfortable with "better," a better that didn't contain the elements of my fulfilling home. With my focus on the next threat, my life was no longer mine to enjoy.

My days were steadily becoming moments weighed on a scale, each experience measured as threat or possible-next-threat. This judgement often replaced joy and the burden of judgement mitigated or replaced my trust.

In this way, no-longer-trusting develops. When we *don't see how* what we are experiencing can possibly fit into and integrate with our *understanding* of life-with-our-treasures, we often become overwhelmed. Without space for conversation and realization, we begin to base our lives on these events. Instead of reaching for our treasures, we begin making choices based on experiences about what we don't want.

> Judgement often replaced joy and the burden of judgement mitigated or replaced my trust.

So, when we feel overwhelmed, being over-whelmed signals us to reach for help. On that night, in those moments when I was separated from the clarity and support that would offer relief and help me through the crisis, I grasped for what was closest. What I used to pull myself through was neither clarity nor relief. Rather, there in the backseat of the car, I was grabbing onto the very threat that was overwhelming me and pressing trauma into the palm of my hand.

> We begin making choices based on experiences about what we don't want.

And so, as I grasped, tightening my grip—pressing threat's juices through my fingers to taint all that I would attempt to nourish myself with—I was actually holding on firmly to the very same threat that was overwhelming me. The resulting trauma replaced any ally that I had so desperately hoped to find.

In this way, I began and have continued in my relationship with threat and the trauma that always follows. And while I argued that I was strong enough to take it, that I could bounce back, threat had entered my understanding and would define my experiences; grasped tightly there in my hand as if it would save me, I held onto trauma without question.

> *In perpetual threat, we are fighting Against one another for a survival that we can't freely enjoy.*

I joined the people on the cliff's edge. In perpetual threat, we are there fighting Against one another for a survival that we can't freely enjoy.

Where do your treasures spend their time?
Do you know where they are?
How do they interact in your life?

LIFE WITH TRAUMA

Even as the world we live in becomes increasingly violent, the first threat we experience is rarely as profound or dramatic as murder. However, at some point, we experience a threat and trauma is established as one of our choices. It is possible to recognize the beginning of the relationship: In that moment when we begin moving Against what feels overwhelming and unsafe, we have begun. We have started moving Against life even as we struggle to find a way to survive in it. We replace our own guidance with our distrust as we react to threat.

> We start moving Against life even as we struggle to find a way to survive in it. We replace our own guidance with our distrust as we react to threat.

What experiences threaten your sense of security? Of belonging? What fills the place where you would live freely? What lives in the space between you and your life?

31

As a child, even before I could read, I was told timeless tales. Poems like Eugene Field's *The Duel* were read to me by my mother:

THE DUEL

The gingham dog and the calico cat
Side by side on the table sat;
'Twas half-past twelve, and (what do you think!)
Nor one nor t'other had slept a wink!
The old Dutch clock and the Chinese plate
Appeared to know as sure as fate
There was going to be a terrible spat.
(I wasn't there; I simply state
What was told to me by the Chinese plate!)

The gingham dog went "Bow-wow-wow!"
And the calico cat replied "Mee-ow!"
The air was littered, an hour or so,
With bits of gingham and calico,
While the old Dutch clock in the chimney-place
Up with its hands before its face,
For it always dreaded a family row!
(Now mind: I'm only telling you
What the old Dutch clock declares is true!)

The Chinese plate looked very blue,
And wailed, "Oh, dear! What shall we do!"
But the gingham dog and the calico cat
Wallowed this way and tumbled that,
Employing every tooth and claw
In the awfullest way you ever saw —

And, oh! How the gingham and calico flew!
(Don't fancy I exaggerate—
I got my news from the Chinese plate!)

Next morning, where the two had sat
They found no trace of dog or cat;
And some folks think unto this day
That burglars stole that pair away!
But the truth about the cat and pup
Is this: they ate each other up!
Now what do you really think of that!

(The old Dutch clock it told me so,
And that is how I came to know.)

—Eugene Field

Nursery rhymes and picture books began preparing me for what was "true," for that moment when I "came to know" for myself that what had been told to me was indeed real.

Although still today, while some of our world is crying out "with its hands before its face," others are "employing every tooth and claw, In the awfullest way you ever saw—"

Some of us are watching through fingers drenched in trauma. Some of us are reporting about those who—made from differing patterns of the same cloth—"ate each other up." Doing what we have been taught from the crib, we live roles that support this story. From our place at the table, we organize the world around us.

As part of this work, I too began reacting for self-preservation. I began learning to move Against something "out there" to protect the treasures "in here." I quickly found ways to react with my own Against ... Against what was threatening and Against myself. Shame, blame, opinion, justification, should, and hiding joined with threat, taking seats at my table ... I changed who I was in order to accommodate threat and its allies, in order to continue in this environment that I was now helping to create.

> From our place at the table, we organize the world around us.

This is the trauma. We begin living with the threat to who we are, to our treasures.

Threat enters through many doors. It may come on the voice of someone who loves us. It can arrive in a look. Threat can be delivered with a blow to the back. Each of us has had our own moment—that moment when we come to understand that we can't continue as we had been. The moment when we put our treasures in the chest for safe-keeping.

The result is trauma.

We have replaced our treasures with threat—we have begun surviving.

The reason is incredibly simple: We have replaced our treasures with threat— we have begun surviving.

This is what I did: I simply began moving Against life *by moving Against myself,* in an attempt to preserve some breathing room. Limiting my possibilities and leaving my breath shallow, I was barely left with space to live. (Remember? My feelings were now in the closet and trauma had begun filtering my responses to my life. Threat had moved in and I made a big space for it at my table.)

Let's take a moment to talk about who we are, here under the evening sky, sitting together, the frogs, the fire, me with you. When the wind shifts, dancing fire's smoke, I smell the damp of night and I feel the breeze across my face, bringing my hair around to play in my eyelashes.

Our senses, our amazing senses, bring intricate realizations of where we are. Our senses are available to tell us about our world, a world that isn't steeped in trauma and doesn't threaten. Our senses can let us know that we're part of the opportunities around us...that we belong. Like the cat who came to listen to my stories, our senses are listening as life snuggles in with us.

In this exchange with life, we are actually taking our place, living center stage with a bounty of information. Our senses are listening to our world and then humming with the stories of our experiencing. In this exchange with life, we write our intimate stories.

Let's dive into that creamy experience, perhaps like whipping cream with just a hint of vanilla and rose water. If you'd like to, write a sense-experience that feels lovely, maybe a warm bubble bath, perhaps sun saturating a ripe tomato...letting your touch form your words, your image of that warm feeling inside.

What experiences threaten your sense of security?
Of belonging?
What fills the place where you would live freely?
What lives in the space between you and your life?

If you'd like to, write a sense-experience that feels lovely, letting your touch form your words, your image of that warm feeling inside.

WHAT TRAUMA DOES NEXT

I t's imperative to me that I know and feel who I am. And, that I am here speaking with you. Part of my life's true meaning is being here in this star-filled breeze of autumn's warm touch, speaking in the hushed tones and boisterous exclamations of our acknowledged treasures.

As we consider trauma, an excruciating experience that is fastidious and fascinating in its movements and abilities, let's go back inside. I have something to show you.

When I was a kid, we did this experiment, putting celery stalks in glasses of water and adding food coloring. I've done that here. The first glass has a stalk of celery in water. The next one also has blue food coloring that I added this afternoon; the blue has begun to absorb into the stalk. In this glass I have obviously added red food coloring and it has moved through the entire stalk. In each instance, the celery has begun absorbing what is in the glass.

While we move back out to the fire, let's consider how trauma moves. It travels through us, coloring our perceptions like the dye moves through the celery. It colors how we see

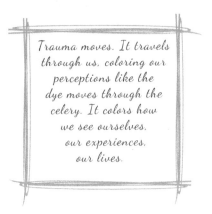

Trauma moves. It travels through us, coloring our perceptions like the dye moves through the celery. It colors how we see ourselves, our experiences, our lives.

ourselves, our experiences, our lives. But this dye does not only move through our understanding of life since the time we began our relationship with trauma. Like red food coloring, trauma impacts the whole of us—changing our understanding of the past as well as coloring our future experiences.

Now that you've traveled with me and my father in the car, you know that the life I was living to that point was rough. What might surprise you is that I had thought life was just fine, that is until trauma changed what I saw. That's the simple truth. I was like the first stalk of celery. I was going along being me, in my own clear water.

There were definitely a lot of things I didn't understand. When things hurt, like when Daddy came to my bed every night, I just went somewhere else while I waited for things to make sense. If I was really angry, I'd put up a fight. If I couldn't figure something out, I'd let it go past—choosing to not participate in the events that I could do nothing to change. There were things that seemed pretty strange, like Mother telling me I'd ruined everything when I'd only just arrived into this world—we actually hadn't even left the hospital. I wondered about these strange things sometimes, like when she brought this up to remind me.

You see, I had my curiosity (one of my treasures) blooming right there in my hand. With my curiosity being nourished in fresh clear water, I found places to explore—in my books, in my yard, and with my friends. I had my laughter, my adventures, my brother to play with and a new baby sister to tell stories, tales of fun, of purple-crayon pies and swings that glided into the clouds. We traveled the world together, exploring and wonder-ing while Mother was resting. I knew how I felt inside, with me. That is where I lived from.

But then, I couldn't see any way to not feel threatened. I had thought, until that night, that— since the people who I lived with were so angry,

41

tired and far away from me—I would just look for more people. But then, when everything became so much more pervasive and violent, I questioned my ability to navigate.

Before that night, I had thought that my way of life was typical.

Robert Louis Stevenson wrote about these same moments—I was sure—in poems about his own life. Although he actually had tuberculosis, I believed he was talking about being home like me, unable to walk in the morning or having too much bleeding to go outside. We were sharing a world and that was fine, in this very special place to have:

THE LAND OF COUNTERPANE

When I was sick and lay a-bed,
I had two pillows at my head,
And all my toys beside me lay,
To keep me happy all the day.
[...]
I was the giant great and still
That sits upon the pillow-hill,
And sees before him, dale and plain,
The pleasant land of counterpane.

—Robert Louis Stevenson
in, *A Child's Garden of Verses*

These words opened places, places of shared space, welcoming me to a life where I understood the world. I especially took great delight in another Stevenson poem about a special friend who stopped by every evening:

THE LAMPLIGHTER

My tea is nearly ready and the sun has left the sky;
It's time to take the window to see Leerie going by;
For every night at teatime and before you take your seat,
With lantern and with ladder he comes
posting up the street.
Now Tom would be a driver and Maria go to sea,
And my papa's a banker and as rich as he can be;
But I, when I am stronger and can choose what I'm to do,
Oh Leerie, I'll go round at night and
light the lamps with you!
For we are very lucky, with a lamp before the door,
And Leerie stops to light it as he lights so many more;
And O! before you hurry by with ladder and with light,
O Leerie, see a little child and nod to him tonight!

— Robert Louis Stevenson
in, *A Child's Garden of Verses*

I looked forward to when I too would grow "stronger" and could then "choose what I'm to do."

But then, after that night on "linens day," I began to think that if that many people could enjoy something so much while I was feeling so very sick, right there in the trees with the world all around, well I wasn't so sure that it would be ok. I wasn't sure I could be ok.

I was, however, incredibly fortunate. I didn't take the experience of that night and make it part of my celery; I didn't infiltrate each cell with red food coloring. I kept my celery (myself) as my own but with just enough doubt to color how I saw life when I was in the other, different, red-dye glass.

I have since figured out that the doubt did not only color what came next; like water, it flowed in all directions at once. So, things that had been strange experiences were now threatening and worrisome. I had to start being on guard and trying. I was afraid for the first time about what would happen next.

Doubting my ability, I began basing how I lived on what someone else was doing, might do, had done. I began using trauma to sort my experiences according to the threat that they might bring, had brought, or did bring. And that, my friends, is how the trauma born from threat seeps in and spreads.

I began living based on what someone else was doing, might do, or had done.

My response became Against those "someone else-s"

> *I began using trauma to sort my experiences according to the threat.*

and so Against myself. Connections and shared lives began falling in a tangle around my ankles, my shiny black shoes now part of the burden that always lurked, like the button that held the strap across my foot—a button I had once thought was pretty.

I have since observed that the threat that each and every one of us experiences, in some form, soaks up and through us. Some people do, however, have a passion that limits the space where trauma can travel within.

> *The threat that each and every one of us experiences, in some form, soaks up and through us.*

There are people who fight Against the trauma, fighting a hurtful system with advocacy work, with caregiving. There are people who work diligently to keep their space intact, following their treasure-based passions—keeping threat at arm's length. It's hard work. Sorting experiences and people according to the threat they may present, fighting Against what life brings, is exhausting to our psyches and our bodies. I joined that fight.

I said that I am grateful. Here's why: I appreciate that I already knew how to care for my spaces. Although I didn't have anyone to talk to about what had happened and although trauma had become my constant companion, I had many more things that had my first priority. The red food coloring was in my celery but I still kept My Celery, My Life. I made a rainbow of celery stalks and I tended and enjoyed each of them. My first relationship was and is with myself. I've met people who have a much different experience.

Before we consider trauma's influences, I'd like to have a bit of quiet time together. Quietly pausing, let's recall how we hold threat in our lives, how we fill the spaces inside of us with experiences from "out there"—while maybe using our passions, maybe using our fears, or our ability to fight as we make a bit of breathing room for ourselves. And let's notice how we fill the spaces around us, filling these spaces, perhaps, with experiences that might somehow help to protect the spaces and treasures we are inside.

Let's move around and get something warm for ourselves. There are lanterns lit and set at the edge of our circle. Take one with you if you'd like. Go ahead and enjoy some warm soup and bread in the kitchen. You'll find paper, pens, pencils, various markers and crayons next to the place settings at the table.

While you're eating or after you've finished, perhaps make some notes—in whatever style suits you—about how you address trauma. How do you survive in places where you feel threat pressing in? How do you respond to being overwhelmed? Do you see yourself taking a stance that strives to protect? Do you let the world work it out while you're tending to other matters?

How do you survive in places where you feel threat pressing in? How do you respond to being overwhelmed?

While many of us practice a bit of each, what are the particular details of passion and trauma in your life? As you live with trauma, how do you respond to threat? How do the things you are passionate about fill the spaces of you? How do the things you fear affect the way you get up in the morning? How does this all fit together?

How do the things you fear affect the way you get up in the morning?

47

When you're ready, we'll meet back here.

How do you hold threat in your life?
How do you fill the spaces inside with experiences
from "out there"?
How do you fill the spaces around you with
experiences that might somehow help to protect the
spaces and treasures you are inside?

How do you address trauma?
How do you survive in places where you feel
threat pressing in?
How do you respond to being overwhelmed?
Do you see yourself taking a stance that strives to
protect? Do you let the world work it out while
you're tending to other matters?

*What are the particular details of passion
and trauma in your life?
As you live with trauma, how do you
respond to threat?*

How do the things you are passionate
about fill the spaces of you?
How do the things you fear affect the
way you get up in the morning?
How does this all fit together?

LIVING WITH TRAUMA
AS THE MAIN CHARACTER

Each of us is a desire thirsting for succulent quench and saturating ease of expression. We are our treasures, treasures that are dancing—our capacity for blossoming lives within. Each bloom of our lives inspires another.

Our passion is a thirst that is satisfying, that lives and thrives—when not absorbed in the parched taint of threat. When we are in our passions, thirst flows; a waterfall quenches in full billowing expression, breathing mist to the clouds, offering frog-current-drench to the muddy soil of nourishing possibility.

I did not continue listening clearly to my desire, to my thirst for quench and flow. I often interrupted my harmony and I frequently stopped tuning myself to my own rhythm. When there was the push of discord, of dishonoring, I learned to listen there and hear that beat. When anything was disrupting so that I felt out of synch, I went to see what might emerge to threaten me.

When I found or stumbled into some jolt or tremor, I'd wrapped it with my voice. As things wafted in on these currents, I was thrown into or left inside of more trauma. When circumstances that left me on arid fields of imbalance and disharmony…I melded into these landscapes.

I learned to focus on what I don't want instead of on what I truly need to crest and flow. So sometimes I forget what I need. I forget that it is the spaces

I learned to focus on what I don't want instead of on what I truly need to crest and flow.

forming letters, those sudden, unforcasted bursts of rain filling open spaces before plopping and splashing, the hush of cloud-filled-sky in full-moon-splendor and sunshine blanketing pine-needle-forestations — river-shimmer-flow where my-imperative-self and her-quenching-need burst forth in dazzle-light-expression of tender kiss on a wrinkled cheek, rainbows in dish soap and the strokes of morning-hair-brushing that untangle sleep. It's imperative, me here with me and yet, from time to time, I'm still absent for my roll call.

I wonder: Have more of your treasures come to mind? Who shows up in your roll call? Who are you in the shower, rinsing bubbles from your hair as you stand naked? Who are you when you're resting? Do you rest in the hush of hearing your pulse's whisper, joining your heart with your voice?

* * * * *

I'm glad we decided to come outside to restoke the fire. I'm glad we are together welcoming energy to dance across the wood in reds, yellows, oranges, blues, and creams ... spectrum warming night's chill and calling our ears with pops and hums. I'm glad we're here together, exchanging our ideas and curiosities, holding ourselves and each other well. Thank you...

Let's take a moment to write down some ways that we nourish ourselves. Let's put stars next to the ones that feel good in our bodies, that feel gentle and nourishing like waking from a nap in the spring's warming sun.

This morning, a dear friend shared a mural she has created. Her handprints are part of the magic that she sings across the paper. As colors move and form with her voice, her excitement and wonder fill the page and also the space that I'm in … an experience of visiting her exhibition, moving with the voices she has gathered there, voices that are filling my senses with color and laughter and anguish, canvas and pigment as imperative expression.

If you would like to, I encourage you to bring your print to the image you are creating. What does your print feel like? What colors do you express with? Do you paint, draw, form words? I encourage you to invite your pizazz to rise up, creating colors and hues of what nourishes you.

I've noticed that what we feed ourselves *with* has quite often been classified and arranged into groups, sorted in our struggle to survive between the "good" and the "bad." Like the food we eat, our lives have

> *Our lives have become dominated by categories that separate and differentiate.*

become dominated by categories that separate and differentiate.

Broccoli is good but we want sugar. Fat is bad but we love cheese. Behaving and being productive will bring safety but our own new ideas just seem to bring more threat to our experience, where there is never enough time, money, accomplishment, or acceptance.

Around and around. We struggle to keep ourselves on the "right" side. We work to get to the "safe" place—whatever that means in the circumstances where we find ourselves. Fighting for our place, we travel further from what lives within us.

Fighting for our place, we travel further from what lives within us.

As we establish our places within this structure, we continually learn rules for managing. These rules aren't about what we are comfortable with. These categories are not about our discernment or what makes sense to us. This rule -based structure is, however, still different for each person, based on the various categories that we each occupy. While these categories may have a bit of room for moving around, they are truly defining and establish a set of non-negotiable parameters.

The categories all have one common ingredient. Every category is a stipulation. Every stipulation has its basis in threat. Every opinion Every insistence Every burden Every struggle Every (desperate) attempt has its basis in feeling threatened. The result: Moment upon moment of acting Against ourselves,

Against each other, Against life—all resulting in trauma. Every time.

This is because trauma is the only possible result.

Acting Against, trauma is the only possible result.

Situating ourselves to act Against, we take a stance that necessarily establishes parameters. When we put this polarity in front of who we are, we cannot thrive. Surviving becomes an element of every forward step. For, without our clear voices, which can't be wholly contained within these categories, we are not fully showing up. We are, therefore, moving away from ourselves, leaving behind all that we truly need for breathing, speaking, seeing, hearing, feeling, loving, thriving and flourishing.

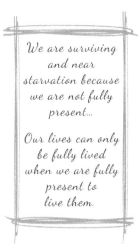

We are surviving and near starvation because we are not fully present...

Our lives can only be fully lived when we are fully present to live them.

We get by. We are surviving and near starvation because we are not fully present; we cannot be truly fed and nourished by anything that is happening without us. These lives, our lives, can only be fully lived when we are fully present to live them.

"Living" is thriving and our lives are actually about expressing ourselves. Yet, here we are moving Against, moving with threat by upholding categories and reiterating trauma, circling in the red dye that is defining our stalks as its own.

What we do is survive to express the threat that we have learned.

> *We survive to express the threat that we have learned.*

And when the parameters become too tight, when our held-in and unheard voices start to suffocate us, we find a way to express through our established roles.

Some of us express ourselves by managing the experiences of others. In this way we may be maintaining categories while safeguarding our own roles and spaces. Some of us find a place to hide from expectations. Some of us find a rope or a gun because we simply have to express ourselves, moving within the given categories that we have each allowed and have all in some way accepted.

All of us.
Repeatedly.
In some way.

It might be clarifying to write down some ways you live in relationship to the threats you experience.

What ways do you have to help ensure your survival?

Have more of your treasures come to mind? Who shows up in your roll call? Who are you when the shower is rinsing foaming bubbles from your hair as you stand naked? Who are you when you're resting? Do you rest in the hush of hearing your pulse's whisper, joining your heart with your voice?

Take a moment to write down some ways that you nourish yourself. Put stars next to the ones that feel good in your body, that feel gentle and nourishing.

Bring your print to the image you are creating. What does it feel like? What colors do you express with? Do you paint, draw, form words?

TRAUMA AS THE DIRECTOR

My experiences may seem extreme to you. They may seem typical. You might not have a place for believing them. Experiences may be thought of as extreme because they have been until recently, in general, unknown, excused, justified, or hidden from shared perception. Experiences of being stopped on the side of the road and beaten. Being called into question for earning a living, for learning, for smiling. Being shamed for thinking in circles instead of lines, for seeing a different possibility or knowing a different answer.

Fighting and resisting don't actually bring safety.

Questioning and guarding, we often stand Against what looks different. Yet, fighting and resisting (to maintain a space) don't actually bring safety. Only our treasures bring security, creating a space of belonging and care. The only space we thirst for is a place to breathe, inhaling and exhaling ourselves out loud.

Yet, we work Against. Our red dye moves through, dominating what you and I see in the glass. We see a glass of red celery— of threat—trauma emerging and leafing out, red swirling in the water.

> *The only space we thirst for is a place to breathe.*

We have taken in these lessons that diminish us because we are intimate with threat. We find it in the morning when we wake up and we take it with us as we find our way to the kitchen. We sprinkle it in the air so that we will breathe it in, because we can't forget. It isn't "safe" to forget.

So, whether dodging the reprimand of an adviser in graduate school, or smiling at the lady in church who feels creepy and wants a hug, or clenching teeth to not scream while Mother goes to find another hairbrush since the first one broke (because of me and not because she had been beating me with it), in each and every case, we are playing out the struggle in the same basic way.

We struggle to mitigate the threat. This struggle is acted out in our experiences, acted out in whatever way we find in the moment. We seek to grab the safest path through the current threat—but this is only a safety that exists relative to our own relationship with trauma. This safety is a move Against a threat; it is not a safety that nourishes. This safety does not afford wellbeing.

I've watched the story rewind and repeat. I've felt myself go down the same road that leads to the same railroad track where the same train barrels down on top of me. So I've searched for a better stance, a cleverer tactic, a safer person, a bigger risk to prove that I'm ok. Some folks pick up a cigarette, a drink, a needle, a literal or verbal gun, hairbrush, rope.

I watched my father. I watched his father, his brothers. I watched them rape me, and I watched them threaten and avert their eyes from each other. I watched each person find a role and throw hate at the others.

I was talking with a friend about our fathers, about their lives, lives informed by the war fought in Korea. I have talked with friends whose parents' lives were redirected or ended by World War II. I've spent time with soldiers, men who each came silently home with crisis as their reference point and trauma as their uniform.

They were met by families, families for whom threat was also a meaningful tool, a way forward that they shared and knew how to implement, a tool that they had for teaching their children, a way that they knew for expressing life. Each person had their own expression and yet, each had trauma for use in the environment that was home.

I have grown up with their children. I hear the voices that we use to speak some echo of their experience. And before these wars, these experiences, these threats, there were others and before those, there were more…

I watched the story again in the civil rights movement—a man standing before me in his pressed green shirt, leaning on the mantel and telling me that if I believed in equality, I wouldn't lock my car door and I'd give him my gun. People in the room were a bit shaken but fifty years later, I saw a t-shirt with the words, "Not Less." I've never seen a t-shirt with the word, "Enough."

Other times we search for relief and nourishment in non-violent interaction. For a bit of one-on-one, we have met on a "basketball court" —a hoop secured on the garage wall where we shared a game.

I've watched the eyes of my peers, soldiers returning from Vietnam who still sift the sands of their stories through battered fingers. I've read the story in book after book. Circumstances change as the storyline repeats. I have been seated with friends in coffee houses, classrooms, meetings, on curbs, on beaches, in cold cars and over hot plates of food asking, demanding, crying, "But what can I do?"

And I devour stories where the heroine walks out of the storyline and says, "I have something else to do."

There are people whose inner lives need to be expressed, red dye or no.

Yet, what we express contains the dye that has colored the space, that fills our vision and directs our options—we are these people. We build walls— walls for prisons, corpora- tions, nursing homes, and

What we express contains the dye that has colored the space— we are these people.

schools, and then we move into these structures— searching for expression and relief from the burning that the red dye is pouring down the walls.

We move in futile and fatal circles as lava flows and seeps to our bones and directs the callouses on our toes to march forward in anguish...even as we care for and support each other with love and its possibility.

And we are people using the space between the letters to write our own voices, breathing our own particles, nourishing ourselves with food that is changing the red to orange, then yellow then celery-green—each breath with less Against, less threat, less trauma offered, received, and exchanged, a little less on each breath.

Who are we? Why do we seem to move so differently in these our moments?

Who are we, these people who minimize the burden of threat and the permeating trauma that goes with it?

Simply put...we are these people too.

We are people who can begin to realize our own human capacity. We can learn to recognize our voices as imperative and we can announce our choice. We can

> *We are people who can begin to realize our own human capacity.*

learn to shift our focus, to use our time and energy on our own behalf.

We can begin fighting less, hiding less from the threat that takes up so much of the air and colors the water. Ours are lives that can seek out new waters and find ways of shedding dye.

Ours are lives that can seek out new waters and find ways of shedding dye.

We are sitting together, we are going for walks. We laugh at a bird, we smile with a friend, we let light come through our eyes when we meet a stranger. We stop being brave for a moment so that we can listen to how we truly feel. We watch a sunrise together. We find work that we enjoy and create nourishing interactions that open our treasure chests and excite our minds.

Each person has a personal relationship with trauma. Each person, each of us, we are all living these, our lives. Each of us is finding our own way. And each of us has an opportunity to choose and choose again.

Each of us has an opportunity to choose and choose again.

For most of my life, I sought to create a space in the world where I wouldn't feel threatened. I sought a place where light would fill the air and hold grace and possibility and more joy. I gave love and offered care, and I contributed curiosity and inspiration. I planted flowers and opened homes where we met around the dinner table to share lasagna, wine and the day, a birthday cake, a cup of tea.

I have also brought threat, hammering the table, pointing out the lack, the starvation, the terrorizing moments—while offering to hold a hand through that terror. I admit that I did what I did from love, and I also loved and acted from threat and with threat, repeating loudly all that my trauma held and may still hold.

When I realized there was a choice, I changed my commitment. I am changing my relationship with trauma and I continue to look for the fresh opening. Seeking the food in my core, I am nourishing each next moment with the voice that is my life. I am realizing what Against looks like and learning to step aside, no longer making myself vulnerable to threat and trauma.

> *I am realizing what Against looks like and learning to step aside, no longer making myself vulnerable to threat and trauma.*

This might be a time to write down your choices, your ways of being present in the world. Which of these choices nourish you? Circle what feels nourishing, perhaps putting stars next to what feels particularly brave and putting smiles next to what feels deeply self-honoring.

SIDE BY SIDE, LIVING WITH TRUTH

As we move through our lives, we find ways to live with threat; in this way, we are saturating ourselves in experiences of trauma.

I've noticed so many differing relationships with trauma. Naturally, we are all unique; with trauma as our base, we form our relationships based on what we learn and need. Yet, trauma is a result of feeling threatened and threat isn't that complicated. Threat is simply struggling to survive.

> *Trauma is a result and threat is simply struggling to survive.*

There are some frequent responses to threat that I've noticed.

Some people believe that threat is a fact of life.

When threat is understood to be a necessary part of life, I've seen people simply learn and incorporate

> *Some people believe threat is a fact of life.*

the rules. In this way we might be doing our best to maintain a place within the system of threat. I've noticed how, again, this looks a bit different for each of us. We may all have a part in this to a greater or lesser extent.

Some of us give ourselves to the task at hand, holding the extreme edge of inhumane behavior. Our society has a clear "threat" label for these people who are actually an imperative part of the threat spectrum. For, in order to have threat as a "fact of life," we require folks who obviously go around putting red dye in glasses. These actions fill a need in our threat-based system.

In order to not feel over-run by the very system that we are maintaining, we hold these particular individuals accountable for their role in this system. While this is useful for control and defining order, segregation is also useful as a way of separating ourselves from our own roles in this system. We do this by setting apart the criminals and perpetrators, protesting that this extreme behavior is not something in which we actively participate.

Now obviously I am not saying that, for example, murder and rape are a good idea or humane. These behaviors are, however, an integral part of the social system that we all support and maintain.

Therefore, we contribute to and support the very circumstances that we blame people for upholding in the spectrum we are creating.

People are held accountable for their behavior while another role is praised—"We aren't that." And, although a designated and formidable part of our society acts "immorally" and "unlawfully," these individuals are also experiencing the very same threats that result in the very same trauma, as Against dominates their lives as well. Yet, some of us hold ourselves "above" and "apart from" the extreme behaviors that we are in actuality relying upon.

Simply put: If there is a "Best" then a "Worst" must exist for comparison, both equal components of trauma and the experience of threat, our treasures deeply buried. We are maintaining this, this that is in actuality an imbalance, a teetering. We maintain the threat by standing Against what we don't want.

> *Simply put: If there is a "Best" then a "Worst" must exist for comparison, both equal components of trauma and the experience of threat.*

If someone exemplifies the "Best" of human expression then we require someone who will stand on the opposite side, who will set the example that makes it clear who is better and who is worse. If "evil" didn't exist, we would have no measure for "saintly" behavior.

When no longer threatening ourselves and each other—not even those we are threatened by—trauma won't have a place.

To be clear, I am not saying people would stop doing lovely things. Quite the opposite. When we stop painting inhumane behavior into the spectrum, when we are no longer threatening ourselves and each other— not even those we are threatened by—trauma won't have a place, will no longer perpetuate inhumanity.

So in a woods where traumatized people take threat as a necessary fact of life, that mob is expected to act inhumanly. That group of people holds the far end of the spectrum and not only do the rest of us *not* provide a way off of that ledge that they are backed onto—we need them to stay right where they are doing just what they are doing.

You may be thinking, "Wait a minute! How can that possibly be true? I certainly don't condone lynching. I don't participate in that."

Yes, of course, I agree that not each person is in this extreme part of the spectrum. Each person does, however, uphold the extreme-band-width.

The experience I told you about was possible because we are each integral parts of the whole and at this point of human existence, murder and gang murder are part of what we support. This is how we live, surviving. Whether we are the clock on the wall or the cat with pieces flying around the room, we are all part of the "duel" and we are each traumatized in our role.

We are all part of the "duel" and we are each traumatized in our role.

An instance is warfare. Wars are mob murder—upheld and esteemed, considered a necessity for wellbeing. This actually requires us to, again, set up extreme threat situations in order to maintain the spectrum we are defending, using our stance Against to maintain our structures and categories.

Further, war is paid for with large amounts of what we say we value (human life, currency that represents value, funds that are drawn away from other activities that we say we value); if the war of threat no longer existed these resources would simply be available for a plethora of other activities. War results from our perpetuation of threat, which then manufactures more trauma, including creating imbalance for the planet itself. It simply does.

War is an example of professional, institutionalized threat that is condoned by many. The resulting trauma is justified when enough people identify a particular threat. It is then that murder is consciously exonerated to maintain the spectrum.

Once these decisions are made, the red dye simply flows to become a part of all aspects of the celery, that which we call our society and the people who comprise it. This is just one example from our system of threat, which is thriving as we maintain our relationship with trauma. Our system of threat is thriving while we are struggling to survive.

> *Our system of threat is thriving while we are struggling to survive.*

The lynching is not different. That man was chosen as a threat because his skin did not match the white skin of his murderers. He called out for his children's safety because they too shared his skin color. He was threatened and ultimately murdered because the spectrum we are incorporating into our lives once again requires someone to be "less" so that someone else can have "more."

And that spectrum is so well established that each of us feels the threat that we would be to the spectrum if and when we might fail to uphold our roles. I was a small child. He was one man in a mob. The strength and the power were not in our hands. Each of us were, however, necessary parts of the larger spectrum...of lives lived in threat. As a child, I was taken off guard.

Until then, I had believed that the brutality I was experiencing was particular to my family; I did not yet realize that trauma is not particular, it affects us all.

> Trauma is not particular...
> it affects us all.

Yet, I had my books. I taught myself to read *Harold and the Purple Crayon* by Crocket Johnson. I was (and remain) absolutely sure that as human

81

> *I was (and remain)
> absolutely sure that
> as human beings,
> we can pick up
> our crayons and
> draw the adventures
> we choose.*

beings we can pick up our crayons and draw the adventures we choose.

Although I certainly didn't understand the picture my parents had drawn me into, I never questioned my ability to color outside the lines they drew. I had myself, my treasures. I also had my tree and my grass and my cat. There were other things to draw than the picture that my parents were creating. I just had to figure out how and where.

That night as our eyes locked, I knew he was dying and neither of us could change the story. I also knew I had to get into my father's car and ride back home. I realized that the picture my parents were creating was part of a much bigger picture than I had imagined.

In fact, it wasn't until many years later that I recognized that I was being trained to draw the same pictures. I was being taught to follow the rules of the extreme edge of the spectrum and to create the world accordingly.

Like Harold with his purple crayon, I was allowed to go for a picnic in the trees—there were simply murderers there along with three kinds of delicious pie. (If anyone had realized what I was up to, that I was in the process of creating another option, I'm sure I wouldn't have been allowed to read. Many people are not allowed this opportunity that I was able to give myself.)

In my space in the backseat of the car, as the orange cigarette burned and the smell of urine wove through the acrid scent of murder, I slowly reached for and found that rock that sits below my belly, that place inside where I can sit and be still. The man was dead. I knew that. I was breathing. I had to find a way to keep myself.

Another thing was clear; the man hanging from the tree had a rock too. He had his rock when he died. I could see that he did. The men in white sheets, my daddy, they had a different look that peered out from their sheets, a look that came from a different kind of rock. Theirs seemed to be burning them up like an exploding volcano.

I had begun my relationship with trauma. I was overwhelmed by threat and I made a conscious decision. Although I soon recognized that red celery was now at my table, it would not be my only color. If I had to, I would just die with my rock but I would never let hot lava burn up all the fineness. I would not base my life on trauma.

It was then that I learned how to find my rock in times of crisis. Eventually I found people who lived with less trauma guiding them, who called on threat less often. As part of this book, I will share more of my experience in order to make obvious the many ways that trauma interrupts our thriving, regardless of our individual role. It is my hope that this clarity will bring our world drama into focus, making clear the prominent role that threat and Against play in our struggle to survive.

> Trauma interrupts our thriving, regardless of our individual role.

FINDING MY ROCK

My mother told me that she resented me, right from the start. I argued about this for a long time and wanted it to not be true. She did, however, move as though motherhood were a heavy weight soldered to her neck. I was the first of three burdens that she felt were threatening to pull her down, to drown her in whatever she was fighting Against. She survived and fought with tremendous skill, tirelessly seeking.

My father, on the other hand, actually reacted with compassion in moments when I experienced pain that he had not been directly instrumental in creating. He often said that he hated his life and by the way that he moved in the world, I soon came to recognize that he didn't see much in his hands beyond trauma. Threat is all he believed he'd been given. It's what he was able to find and it's what he knew to offer.

So, when I came home from the hospital as a newborn and I wet and I cried, he began teaching me how to stop threatening him with the smell that he hated and the noise he could never express. It worked. Only once in the eighteen years I was there did I cry out when he raped.

As the pain continued day after day, I stopped nursing. I stopped moving. I was put in a children's hospital, in the newborns' isolation ward. I had a fever and the doctor had no idea what was wrong with me.

I obviously didn't die of starvation and my fever receded before the heat damaged my body. The staff must have provided intravenous nourishment and fever relief but I didn't move for a long time.

While I was left alone to find my way, I found my rock and I sat there. I didn't start to move until I was sure of my rock, sure of that place inside where I felt like me—unhurt, quiet, a soft blue mist that has lights and laughter and my treasures. Me whole and safe. Then my parents took me back home.

Years later on that autumn night among the trees, with threat rummaging around to touch everything I knew, I found my rock, my place, and myself. I found the blue mist and the lights. I put my laughter in my pocket where threat couldn't get it, and I took a nap in the backseat of the car. I would, however, spend many hours reviewing the story.

I had ironed the sheet. (The fact that I didn't know what I was doing occurred to me much later.) The man was dead. No one talked about it and I wasn't going to talk about it either.

Somewhere I found the courage to be quiet, to sit, to listen to my voice as I sat on my rock.

Jacque Nelson beautifully describes this process to inner place, to self, in her poem, *Bravery*:

BRAVERY

Sometimes we have to be brave enough to not be brave.
To instead collapse a little, or a lot, and let the dam break.
To give ourselves, for the moment, to the thoughts that life
is pointless and painful and makes no sense to our
tormented, stressed or shattering hearts.
That being happy about anything
feels ignorant and vague.
To deeply feel the sharp edge of grief
that dulls our everything into colorlessness.
And drowns our once vividly felt
magic and light out of our expressing.

Sometimes we have to be brave enough to not be brave.
To instead let ourselves be held by others whose arms,
words and sincerities somehow know how to wrap us in a
gentle warmth even when we are kicking and screaming
in our current inconsolableness.
And even when we just want to run away
to a place and experience
that doesn't exist anymore because
the life "this place" that was
is slowly evaporating or has already moved
beyond our touch.
And ... when we feel far too vacant to notice the presence
or summon the presence of self to openly embrace
compassion's arrival.

Sometimes we have to be brave enough to not be brave.
To instead simply allow our inhale to move in its natural
tandem with our exhale.
To let that be enough.
To let it be absolutely enough for today
and maybe a string of tomorrows.
To lie in our own arms and breathe our own breath
there in the pause.
The important pause with self in the
midst of the unfathomable.
Being brave enough to not be brave.
Allowing ourselves to innately understand that
sometimes not being brave is
the bravest thing we ever do.

—Jacque Nelson

I reached for comfort and place inside, where my treasures kept me company. There was my rock and there were books.

> There is no sliding scale of threat, only in the significance of the trauma that we experience.

The books said "written by" people and the stories I read didn't end in lava. So, I also became another kind of brave. I began looking for people who make stories with crayons instead of white sheets. That decision kept threat off my rock and trauma from infiltrating all of my story.

As people who harm others, we are standing with those whom we harm. There on the edge of the cliff, you'll find us side by side. We are mutually trapped and on the verge of destruction. There is no sliding scale of threat, only in the significance of the trauma that we experience. If any particular members of the spectrum fall into the chasm, more of humanity will be moved to the inhumane edge to occupy the space.

This truth is threatening when we believe that we have no choice that will stop the progression. And while it is certainly painful as we open and focus our eyes, we can recognize—pain has already been carved deeply into this story, we as humanity have been feeling it all along.

For, while we are gradually dying in a drama,

For, while we are gradually dying in a drama, we have grown into our suffering.

we have grown into our suffering. As we live the roles that we play, we grow used to our place and develop the skills of survival.

We are tangled with harm in devastating trauma. Yet, we have a sense of place in the spectrum of threat.

What we can do is admit what is happening. We can decide to commit to something new, even when we have no idea what that might be. We can't make a choice, however, when we don't realize what it is that we're doing. Or when we simply silence the threat.

Covid-19 slowed life down a bit. This slowing down has shifted the spectrum of trauma. Humanity has slowed down just enough to realize being chased, has slowed just enough to turn around and look at what has been going on. We have been jarred and we are calling on one another to admit the lives we are creating and to move beyond this overwhelming realization.

We are calling on one another to admit the lives we are creating and to move beyond this overwhelming realization.

We have an opportunity to hear what has been said and what is being said, to listen before we speak into the hushed.

The spectrum has shivered. It is still shivering and it's been shivering for long enough that the colors are slowly re-orienting themselves. Glasses are starting to fall over. The red dye is mixing a bit with other colors. We're creating mud.

Attempts to maintain the lines and control the story are becoming less stable, some are already losing their connection. As more and new voices are speaking, we are realizing that new connections are possible. We are looking for a crayon and a piece of paper, no longer willing to stand in a glass and have the existing spectrum be what colors our lives, the dye of threat dominating. We are beginning to be curious, to wonder about new choices in our relationship with trauma.

We can't commit to new lives, we can't even create truly different stories without admitting to the story we've been upholding. Remember the red celery? The red dye has permeated the cells, the very fibers of our stalks.

As we start to see and to hear, to speak and to listen, our task is to recognize what things are still of value and what we no longer need as part of our chosen panorama of colors.

> *When we stop acting brave and start bravely noticing what the spectrum is and how we uphold it, then we can honestly choose and begin creating purely from our treasures.*

While threat is moving in the fibers of our being, we are systematically required to find a limited place where we will live. But, as stated in these few words from Emily Dickenson's poem #214 (530):

> You cannot fold a Flood –
> And put it in a Drawer –
>
> —Emily Dickenson
> in *Final Harvest, Emily Dickenson's Poems,*
> Thomas H. Johnson, ed.

Although threat has a long and traumatic reach, it cannot eliminate us without our participation. So, it has formed an incredible bond. This bond is intricately woven. We have become convinced that we are in the process of writing the dramas we desire. We haven't noticed that we've folded our Floods (or some part of ourselves). Putting our passions in Drawers, we are left to survive our lives.

We have come to believe that even though we've ignited threat, we haven't been relegating our lives to a small glass with a bit of red dye.

In truth, however, we are being fed and driven, not by who we are but by who we become when we fold our passion and "put it in a Drawer," substituting survival for our inner spark.

> Our lives are being fed and driven, not by who we are but by who we become when we substitute survival for our inner spark.

In our roles as perpetrators, we find ways of upholding threat and maintaining trauma. When we are in our roles as victims, we often find the receiving end of trauma too difficult to endure. We may agree to move in self-preservation, thereby joining those who inflict the threat.

Sometimes we differentiate ourselves by disintegrating, while at other times we act as sorters, separating life into categories and clarifying the parts we are to play. Sometimes we strive to contain the threat, at other times to ease or dilute the trauma. Most of us play some role in each of the variants.

As traumatized individuals, we go to the store. We carry home cases full of glass jars, vats of red dye, and regular installments of fresh celery. Then, while dealing with our own trauma, we begin to order our minds to mitigate threat—organizing our jars and distributing the contents accordingly. Within the spectrum that we are creating, a system emerges that seems to lessen the trauma by controlling the threat ... often to the point of convincing ourselves that it isn't even present in its inevitability.

Sometimes this doesn't work. Sometimes a way out is needed. Suicide or murder become options for some people. When this happens, we—as sorters and organizers—panic. Our structured order has been disturbed and trauma deepens, often becoming more firmly lodged. We reorder our need for distance and space from threat by maintaining ever clearer boundaries and/or retreating.

As threatened people, we have become partners with our trauma. In a desperate move, we search in breathless fear for some way to survive. Often, we share vapors of memory, memory of what we sometimes wished, what we longed for and what we longed to keep. We talk about our wondrous light, lit each evening to shine with the moon in star-filled skies. We may recall smiles shared and nods exchanged. We search for these windows to move through so that we can leave behind an arid wasteland of banished self.

But, if we maintain our stories in this relationship with trauma, if we choose to continue finding solace in our place between time and tradition— a place that marks time by the clock, hands over our faces—then we will maintain the spectrum, the structure that creates threat and proliferates trauma.

> *If we choose to continue finding solace in our place between time and tradition, then we will maintain the spectrum, the structure that creates threat.*

So molten lava must continue to form and pour forth. From inequality to global warming, it must wall in the them-s and the our-s, the they-s and the their-s, the she-s and the he-s, the us-s and the we-s.

Then when we begin free fall and are grasping, flailing about to stop our plummet over the edge, we will again grasp trauma's hand, accept our place in threat's spectrum and choose what our next roles will be in the drama of Against.

And

Yet…here

Softly, in whispers of calm relief, I welcome you back.

I welcome you to a seat here. I have my treasures in my lap—blue of the sky, purple of a pansy with its bright yellow face shining up, energetic gnat flying in to say, "hello" while hawk perches on my knee. My paintbrushes spell out the spaces between the letters as my hands reach under the bread dough to mingle the scent of yeast and flour with the wafting of rain's mist on a hot summer's night.

Let's pause together here. Let's be "brave enough" together. Let's simply sit together in our own spaces, with our own lap's treasures. Let's be "brave enough" to open…to ourselves…writing the scent that lives here, drawing the pulse you hear, coloring the taste, articulating the sensation, perhaps …here….

Let's be "brave enough" to open...to ourselves.
Perhaps write the scent that lives here, draw
the pulse you hear, color the taste,
and articulate the sensation.

Forming a Bond and Building a Relationship

The kids and I grew. I had grown into my job as Big Sister. I had read to the babies in the crib and I now played with them on the floor, often being left to "take care of things" when Mother left the room. We had grown into a routine. I found ways to maintain myself and watch over my brother and sister.

Sometimes I was dressed up after my hair had been done in a grown-up beauty parlor and Daddy left me with the man with the camera. But he never wrinkled my dress, putting it carefully on the chair. So, when I was back home, Mother stayed calm and we were all relieved that there would be dinner and maybe even dessert.

New experiences brought new adjustments but the routine expanded without changing. Yet, I would learn to be afraid, afraid that someone would recognize me, some guy who had seen those pictures of me.

One day, a grown-up dresser arrived. It had two sides, one for my sister and one for me. And there were two fancy beds with wood by our heads and feet. Our other grandma had sewn new, dark-blue curtains with dolls from around the world and our bedspreads even matched.

It was a very important day. My sister had never slept in a big-girl bed before and I felt my full flood of joy and amazement as we each climbed under our covers. I turned off the new lamp that had a little dolly on a swing, gliding happily along under the pink and white lampshade, there on the stand between us. We said, "Good night" —I'd never done that before!

While my sister quieted to sleep, I waited for Daddy. I felt less afraid if I was awake when he came to see me. But he walked right past me and I started to panic. He went to the other bed and pulled down my sister's sheet.

All of the sirens that had been waiting unnoticed suddenly began to pulse and shriek through my body— "Leave the baby alone." I didn't think I didn't breathe I only screamed and leapt. I was on his back with my teeth grabbing at his shoulder when he reached around and threw me across the room into the dresser. I must have been bleeding when he grabbed me by the waist and took me into the bathroom, when he left my sister alone.

The water hit my face with full force and just before I couldn't gasp, there was air. Then water. Then air. Then water. Then air. Then water. Then my mind moved to watch from across the room as he threw me on the floor and went to bed. (Today, I wonder where he had been, when he learned to do this.)

I was very cold when Mother tried to wake me. When she eventually called an ambulance, she was talking through her teeth, saying that she had no idea what she'd tell the neighbors. I'd never seen her so angry, her hands gripped in fists, "What the hell is wrong with you? Why would you do such a thing?"

Then I was in the corner of a different room that I didn't know. Two doctors were saying they weren't sure. I was blue-colored, sort of like the new curtains and one of them kept pushing on my chest.

Then I knew, I had another choice. Did I want to go back? I felt different. No place hurt and it was quiet, peaceful without the scared feeling. Everything seemed to stop and I was still. The doctors were getting upset and seemed to want me back, although I didn't even know them.

"What would happen to the kids? But it has to get better than this; that's the only way I'm staying."

And then I was breathing. No cold water hitting my face, just shaking. They gave me a robe with teddy bears, "Do they think I'm a baby?" I could go home in the morning, after Mother promised not to leave me alone in the bathtub again until I was bigger. Once I heard that, I found my rock and went to sleep, wondering if I'd made a mistake by coming back. I also began to wonder if I'd been broken. Was that why I was being sent back?

Once I was back home, a pattern emerged that would continue. Mother began pointing out how stupid I was, how I couldn't be trusted, how I caused so many problems. My brother and little sister joined in. My fear for their safety became a great source for ridicule, particularly from my mother. Yet, I also had no expectation of safety or care. I was alone again in the family.

It was decided that I would no longer be left with the kids and, right at that time, new threat was balanced with escape routes; I was old enough to go to the park with the neighborhood kids and I was allowed to join Girl Scouts! I was a Brownie!

I became less careful. When locked in the attic, I would scream as loud as I could. I didn't scream to be released. I screamed to connect. I didn't have any stories to read and it was dark anyway. But there was this wonderful aspect of being locked away by myself. Screaming was a privilege that I was not afforded at any other time; I roared with my whole voice, hearing my frustration and anguish spoken into the world.

I became so strong that I could scream from lunch to supper without losing my voice. I learned how to stay warmer in winter and not move in the summer heat. I was building stamina and learning how to monitor and care for myself.

When I reached middle school, we moved. Although we had a clear routine, my sister was older and bedtime had become even more difficult. When we moved to the bigger house, there was a bedroom for each of us kids. That's when I found out that I was pregnant.

My summer between eighth and ninth grade was spent in a locked closet during the day and in my room at night. Mother told the kids that I was at camp and I had to keep the small television turned to a whisper. I watched every minute of the Watergate trials, thinking that I was pretty grown up to be so involved in such an important event.

One night in August, a doctor came and put a needle in my arm. I don't remember my daughter being born or how we got to the woods. I felt nauseous but the pain was at bay when I was sitting on the ground, the baby screaming in my arms. Then my whole body seized up. The man said it was my own fault, if I'd had a boy it'd be different.

He threw her into a pack of dogs and laughed; he really did laugh, just like a movie. She was gone before I took a breath. They were big dogs and she was tiny. They kept barking for more. I hoped I was going to follow her but Daddy said, "For Christ's sake," picked me up and carried me to the car.

When I could walk, Mother took me to get school clothes and birth control pills, which were given, of course, without an exam: "It's terrible for me. My own daughter can't be trusted, out running around on her own like she does." She called it thyroid medication and along with the continuous doses of penicillin, we went ahead.

Much later, I named her Sara. She had stopped screaming and looked right into me, just before he grabbed her. Human capacity is an amazing life in this world.

Experts say that newborn babies don't know what's happening and don't focus their eyes, but few mothers will doubt that moment. And it

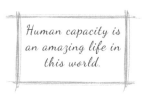

Human capacity is an amazing life in this world.

changed me. She saw me. She saw my rock and I knew she saw it. The man in the woods probably saw me too, since our eyes locked in the same way before he died. But at that time, I had been too young to reach beyond my experience and realize what that feeling was or what it meant.

Sara, on the other hand, had introduced me to the capacity for true, shared love. She opened for me a relationship that wasn't based on, predicated by, or forged in spite of threat. We simply loved each other. That was all and that was enough. I didn't mourn the fact that she might have been allowed to live. I didn't know a world where that would have been possible.

A New Spectrum

Besides the hormonal changes of puberty, childbirth, and birth control, I had this significant new development to integrate into my spectrum. I had shared a feeling with another person that wasn't about struggle or striving. I had a new feeling of possibility. Those nine months and that brief moment with Sara had introduced me to a new kind of love.

And, things were changing again. I had systematically read all of the books in my neighborhood library and I moved to the main branch, borrowing a stack of books at a time. Plus, there was a new school with a new library and new people.

I only attended the middle school for one year. I enjoyed geometry and drama class (something I never imagined I could study) but I was still lost in the past summer's events and their ensuing fog.

While I was attending ninth grade, I spent time on my rock, where I considered my next move. A whole new level of trauma and threat had also brought this incredible capacity to love and be loved. I began to color my own spectrum.

I'm not telling a Cinderella story here.

I am saying that I was older and could be away from it all for an entire night, spending evenings and overnights with friends, going to camp and on trips—it was a miracle that gave me space to be me. I grabbed the chance with both hands and never let go. I met real people who took out their crayons, had ideas, asked me questions, and offered me things to share in that I enjoyed. Where the red dye of threat wasn't the primary color surrounding me, I began to develop a new story.

TRAVELING WITH THREAT

N ow that we've brought our spectrum of threat into conscious focus, let's move around a bit.

While I see humans living on the cliff's edge, it is also true that many of us have found a way to feel safer or less at risk. This is certainly a differing experience for each individual.

Stratification and varying degrees of risk allow for different ways of measuring threat, creating diverse trauma experiences. Some people are able to access lives that have less obvious threat. These people live in ways that illuminate more individuated spectrums, identities, passions and dreams. As Julia Roberts quietly describes in *Pretty Woman*, we don't [all] dream of living lives determined by "the bad stuff." We just

> *Stratification and varying degrees of risk allow for different ways of measuring threat, creating diverse trauma experiences.*

get used to it after a while, then start following it from one choice to the next.

While some lives are given to defining threat and then proving it in one way or another, there are those who establish themselves in other ways. Marge Piercy's poem, *If they come in the night*, depicts an approach that I chose and I've included a few of her words here:

IF THEY COME IN THE NIGHT

(...)

I said, I like my life. If I
have to give it back, if they
take it from me, let me only
not feel I wasted any, let me
not feel I forgot to do some little
piece of the work that wanted
to come through.

Only what we manage to do
lasts, what love sculpts from us ...

—Marge Piercy,
in *Circles on the Water*

This approach is not built on a lesser threat. However, when the focus is different, we do experience the impact differently...even though our passions and choices are still lived waiting for threat to swoop in.

My grandmother on the farm, my "good grandma," my father's mother, lived a bit of this life. To my eyes, she spent a lot of her time on those hugely swollen knees. She gardened. She grew (canned and prepared) all of the vegetables that the family ate and she grew her flowers, there on her knees in the soil. (Although gardens did not seem to bring him joy, my father always had a vegetable and flower garden; when he was in the garden, he did actually seem to be breathing. As for me, I have enjoyed planting flowers and vegetables on every available space of soil that I could.)

Grandma was a devout Catholic. After her husband died from lung cancer, she spent long hours kneeling on wooden floorboards with her elbows propped on the hard wooden seat of a white chair, praying her rosary for his release from purgatory. I had no sense whatsoever that she loved him, she may have. Perhaps like Piercy, praying was her "piece of the work." As far as I could see, most of her life was an answer to the next piece of work that needed to be done.

She smiled when she gardened — I even heard her hum. And I saw her enjoy her church ladies and their time together playing cards. That was when she laughed.

Even though she was by no means warm, nurturing, or playful, she was my rock in the world. My source of care, possibility, gentle touch, and genuine, deeply felt love. After my fifth birthday, whenever there was a long weekend or a vacation from school, I begged to stay with Grandma. I was filled with complete joy and gratitude when I was allowed to go.

It wasn't the sanctuary from my parents that I treasured; that went unnoticed in the complete wonder of being with Grandma. Well, there was also the fact that she lived in the country. With no indoor plumbing or central heating, I was the only grand-child begging for the chance to be with Grandma, although why they all didn't want to play in the creek that ran along the road or explore the forbid-den woods, or help with gathering the eggs is still a mystery to me. The outhouse just smelled like an outhouse; it wasn't really nasty.

The canning pantry in the back of the house was pure gold stacked neatly in jars above the potatoes and onions. Right outside its door was the ringer washer. I'd perch on the stool to watch mashed clothes emerge from the rollers while wood burned in the canning stove, boiling wash water. The funniest thing I'd ever seen was Grandpa's frozen long underwear hanging on the clothesline; I was mesmerized as I watched frozen laundry thaw dry, perched on chairs around the kitchen stove.

The smell of coffee was always lingering just outside the porch door to greet me and when my family intruded by coming along on Sundays, we watched *The Wonderful World of Disney* after dinner. My uncle had purchased the large television; he found the circumstances of the family home, where he still lived, appalling and above Grandma's protesting, he also brought in running water and a washer and dryer after Grandpa died, saying he could no longer live like an animal.

The real magic happened on winter nights when there were fewer chores for her incredibly swollen fingers. Grandma would turn off the light and we would sit next to the furnace in the dining room. It was a big, brown, metal rectangle with a pipe that went up to the bedrooms; the row of tiny blue flames gave off enough heat to keep frost from the walls upstairs where the most glorious Christmas cactus flourished.

Grandma and I sat right up close to the furnace, there in the dining room on one of those straight hard chairs. She held me close as I curled up in her lap. Then Grandma would hum. This was the only warm place I knew. It felt like sitting on my rock and even today my pulse deepens and my breath is fuller just thinking about it. Her love poured over me. My mind and body were peaceful and we'd sleep there through the night.

Grandma told me to *Never Ever* go in the barn. It was the only time she'd ever looked me in the eyes and besides that, I had to promise. So, of course, I was really, really curious. Grandma was cooking. I had watched my uncle and grandfather go in many times. I decided I wouldn't actually "go in" — I'd just be inside for a minute to look around quickly and then I'd come right back out to the yard.

Turns out, the barn was where Grandpa took "his boys," even as adults. When I went in...well, besides being raped, I was cut on some sort of metal farm equipment and that was a problem. By bedtime,

I couldn't focus very well with my eyes; I was shivering, even my teeth. Grandpa hit something really loudly and on one of three times that I ever heard him speak, he growled at Grandma, explaining that if she went for the doctor, he'd kill us both.

In the middle of that night, Grandma carried me to the wheelbarrow where a heavy quilt and a coat were waiting. My legs hung down to the dirt so she had to lift even higher as she somehow maneuvered that single wheel along the rutted gravel roads. I've since gone back to measure the distance. Singing a hymn, she pushed me the two-and-a-half miles to the church.

She pounded and pounded on the door of the small house but the priest only appeared when she informed him that she wasn't leaving. All of the noise had alerted me and when he stood there in his nightgown glaring at Grandma, she explained that I was dying and hadn't been baptized in The church. As he closed the door, she reminded him that it was his job to save souls.

"For Christ's sake," he swore. She agreed and pushed the wheelbarrow into the church. He adorned his bedclothes with vestments, uncovered the baptismal font and Grandma held me while he prayed.

I gasped. My fever broke. There weren't any singing angels or bright lights or anything. Grandma gave folded money from her coat pocket to the priest and we began the long walk back. I was sorry that I still couldn't stand. Grandma told me to hush about that and never ever say a word.

I was in seventh or eighth grade when I overheard my parents talking with quiet words. This drew my attention so I went to listen; an aneurism had burst. I had no idea what that meant when I rushed into the kitchen to ask if Grandma was dying. Father nodded and I told them that I was going to the hospital, "We have to leave now."

As I am writing this, I still blink in amazement. I didn't make such statements and things I requested didn't just happen. But on that afternoon, Mother drove me to the hospital.

Grandma was in a small room in the ICU and I walked past my aunts who were standing next to the bed, without saying anything. I took Grandma's hand and waited for her to turn her head and look at me. For the second time in my life, she looked into my eyes. I said, "I love you, Grandma." She said, "I know." I nodded and squeezed her hand; she turned her eyes back to the wall and I went back to the car to be driven home.

A big part of my outside stability and experience of "true" left that evening; I had to give her back. Since she believed in heaven, I was sure she was there. I was glad no one would scream at her anymore. I was glad that my uncle couldn't hurl the iron at her head and that she wouldn't have to look me over with that sadness in her eyes, checking to see if I was ok as I walked through the door.

I went to sit on my rock for a while.

Beginning in seventh grade, I tutored kids in reading during my lunch hours and study halls. Other days, I worked in the school's office, answering the phone. If something was interesting, I did it. If I could do something that mattered to me, I did. Besides babysitting jobs, I was later also busy writing for the school newspaper in high school and working as stage manager for all the drama productions, while earning every badge in my Junior and Senior Girl Scout handbooks.

Whether I was starting a girls' basketball team or opening TeenMart at the Farmer's Market, so that we kids could sell our creations, when there were people to meet and new things to try, I was there. I went to every camp and on every field trip; I earned money for bus trips to New York City and Washington DC.

Much to my amazement, when I was about to graduate from high school, my mother asked me what I'd like for my graduation present. We had never taken vacations, except to see her mother, but none the less, I immediately announced that I wanted to go to the Grand Canyon.

For the second time in my life, they just did what I asked. My father borrowed a pop-up pull-behind trailer and away we went. I met amazing people in the campgrounds and saw people who wore real cowboy boots. I don't remember the trip itself.

I do remember the Grand Canyon. I had arrived home.

Of all the possibilities I had found beyond the spectrum of my parent's lives, the Grand Canyon told me that going home was actually possible.

Naturally, after that trip, they-who-come-in-the-night still came in many different ways and at unexpected times, but I only counted my moments of exploration. I cared for the life that was left to me and was grateful for every chance because I knew that eventually they would come.

The other time I was handed a dream, I understood the reason. Mother had not been able to complete more than one year of college. She had lost her scholarship and was told to marry because there was no other place for her.

I was very pleased when I wasn't asked *if* I wanted to go to college but only *where* I wanted to go. It meant something to her wellbeing for me to go; she told everyone. After my father stared at me for a long time, he blinked and walked away. I could go.

With my GPA, I was able to choose a small, expensive Quaker school a few hours to the south. Mother found a job as our church's secretary and paid the tuition that scholarships didn't cover. For my personal expenses, I started in a great job at a bookstore.

When August finally arrived, I insisted on leaving a few days before registration, since I was packed and I'd learned that the dorm was open. I was on the Baha'i floor and I found a wondrous community of people in the dorm and on the campus.

Although I was sure that "they" would continue coming for me, I had an incredibly rich experience. Until, of course, the fear of them suddenly appearing became so strong that I had to leave school because I couldn't concentrate.

I couldn't make myself go back to my parents so I moved in with the guy I'd been dating and eventually we were married. I cried through the entire ceremony. I was completely lost, waiting, always waiting. I had nightmares and read wretched books that told stories of threat and permeating trauma.

But there was also my work. My eighteen-month banking career was a lot of fun. I worked in a small branch of the bank after my training. There were three tellers and we became close, getting together on weekends with our husbands. We had a great boss and I was soon opening safe-deposit as well as checking/savings accounts. Everything was going amazingly well until I started having panic attacks. Like my previous job waitressing, I had to quit because I never knew who would walk through the door.

A close friend, a fellow camp counselor from our high school days, told me about a job that she thought I'd love. I became the youngest "houseparent" they'd ever hired. I was actually paid to help women master skills so that they could live independently. I couldn't believe that that was my life. I was very happy. I could work from my rock.

The women were eventually able to live on their own and I began with a new family, a group of men who also welcomed me. We began to share and build the deepest relationships I'd known.

I was feeling great about my life when I realized that I was pregnant. Seven months later, I had a thirty-two-hour labor as my body worked with my terror—I couldn't possibly bring him into this world. I wanted to share so much with him but I saw no way to protect him. Nothing I had learned or done was bigger than the threat, the threat I saw no way to address.

When they brought him to me, I was sick; besides being hungrier than I could have imagined possible, I had pneumonia. Yet when he was put in my arms, I simply unwrapped the blanket and stared at this beautiful person. As tears streamed down my cheeks, I breathed him in, all the way to my rock.

Every time he nursed, I stared down at him, murmured to him, read out loud to him; we began reading A. A. Milne's *Winnie-the-Pooh* on our first day home. This amazing, precious life was in my arms and I gave myself to the wonder of those moments as he grew.

When it was time to go back to work, I couldn't leave him behind. Options opened and we eventually moved into our new home with the four men who had become our family.

Then, when time had passed, when my son moved to his new big-boy bed, I simply shut down. I was sure that I couldn't keep my baby safe; once everyone was asleep at night, I drank Jack Daniels until I passed out, over and over for several weeks. One night when my husband came home from his second-shift job, he poured the last from the bottle into the sink and told me that if I wouldn't talk to him, then in the morning, I had to find help.

As James Baldwin wrote in *The Fire Next Time*,

> To defend oneself against a fear is simply to insure
> that one will, one day, be conquered by it; fears
> must be faced. As for one's wits, it is just not true
> that one can live by them — not, that is, if one
> wishes really to live.

That summer, all of the fears with which I had grown up, which were now a part of me and controlled my vision of the world, rose up like a wall between the world and me...

All that I had distanced myself from, that I had refused to allow, all that was buried under my rock, it all began to circle around asking, "Where will you go now?"

As I sat on my therapist's floor with her, she asked a more interesting question, "Who are you?"

I sat on my rock, waiting for a way forward to become clear. How to function when my "wits" had suddenly, unexpectedly failed? How to turn around and step forward when I had already failed three young lives, three times before? Three babies had been in my care and been hurt, one of them had been eaten. Now, here was this beautiful boy with his own grown-up bed. So, I asked her this question, "What do I do?"

Thankfully, the therapist whose name I had found in the phonebook, the woman with one opening for a new client, had said I could come. Me, the young mother with good health insurance. And although my emotional health seemed to suddenly be so much ash, she had an answer.

She knew what to do next and she brought more tissues when I had to wait in the stairwell because I was too disoriented to drive. She took the tangled and knotted threads of my life that were there wrapped around my legs, and she placed them in my hands. Quietly, undauntedly, she started helping me unravel the mess I had found, all the while clearly proud of me and trusting me implicitly.

So, I slowly and carefully started to put my two worlds in the same sphere—the world I loved and the world I found incomprehensible began weaving together. I slowly let my eyes adjust so that I could focus on the entirety of my life at one and the same time.

When I tried to say that my mother was right, that I was crazy, my therapist told me about other parents. Those parents had also expressed concern, had also sent childhood pictures and written letters explaining that they too had no idea what could have happened to their daughters, daughters who had obviously had wonderful childhoods ("See the beautiful picture?").

"And?" I demanded. She answered firmly, looking into my eyes, "And those parents had it wrong too."

When I tried to convince my psychiatrist that I was broken and had maybe lost my mind as well, he would have none of it. He told me to phone the sheriff's department and ask for a special crimes' detective, confident that others would also know firsthand about my "crazy" world. Over coffee at a restaurant on the outskirts of town, the sheriff wearing a t-shirt and jeans did know the people I named, those who had been there on those nights. He identified the places I'd been taken. He was young, around my age, so I couldn't rationally ask where the hell he'd been if he KNEW.

And when sorting through the threat and trauma became too incomprehensible to live with, my psychiatrist agreed to let me stay in the hospital. So, for a couple of days, while my son was having his weekend at Dad's, I made my environment smaller so that I could breathe again.

When all of the threads were colorfully part of my fabric, woven into their true places, I had my psychiatrist's blessing as I walked on without medication. I stood up from the wheelchair that had been part of my days and had kept me mobile and I finished the college career I'd begun; enjoying books again, I earned degrees in philosophy and in literature as my son and I attended our schools and talked about what we were learning. I came to understand that while I was loving my son with my entire being, he would find his own way and I'd be there with his father to support and marvel as our son grew.

READING THE TREAD OF THREAT
IN TRAUMA'S FOOTPRINTS

Threat unravels the possibility of thriving and provides no respite, reiterating trauma.

Our relationship with trauma reduces our conversations to a barrage that no longer articulates our need for the belonging of presence and connection.

Trauma encompasses our experiences so that survival, fear, struggle, and burden can step in, hiding us from ourselves and from each other. In the sounds of our anger and terror, our wails for recognition and value slide across the asphalt in waves of electrified need, meeting deaf ears but also deafening as they ride perpetual currents of what we don't want or need.

> Our relationship with trauma reduces our conversations to a barrage that no longer articulates our need for the belonging of presence and connection.

However, when our ears are hearing and our eyes are witnessing, the voices of our stories move in their own light. We are able to take a deep breath. In these moments, we can hear the truth of those conversations that threaten our ability to truly live. The searing division that human experience is perpetuating upon itself can be realized.

> *The searing division that human experience is perpetuating upon itself can be realized.*

But when I refuse any power lest that power pour from my eyes in molten fire, when I join the rallying call to stand tall and brace myself against fear, and when, or perhaps especially when that very fear and the struggle to survive demand Against-filled reactions, then the accompanying cloak of trauma continues to saturate my living.

When I had rolled my rock from on top of that seemingly bottomless pit and when, years and sob-filled decades later, I called down into that pit and heard an echo, reassuring me that the evacuation and release had been thorough, even then I was not free.

Burden persisted with each move, sometimes ruling the moment, sometimes successfully moved to the back. Even brushing my teeth was a burden to be carried, a presence that fogged my sight and filled my ears in those moments. I could not hear my own pulsing gratitude for the water flowing from the tap and the flowers caressing the back stoop.

In those strings of moments, burden welcomed more burden as trauma tightened its grasp. I was struggling under the weight of dental floss and toothpaste, dirty dishes and chicken that wasn't thawed. The joy of forks moving with coffee cups in the bubble bath under my kitchen window was lost, lost in the burden of one more chore.

Weighed down and struggling for even the shallowest of breaths, I didn't notice the signs— "Keep Out," "Uneven Terrain," "Slippery Slopes Ahead," "Storm Warning," "You're Dining on Breadcrumbs not Meals." My bully knew her lines and stepped forward with her chorus, "What The Hell Are You Doing? Just Keep Going!"

I stood Against it all. I'd prove that I could win. I'd made it through worse.

Struggle...Survive...Repeat...

I continued inviting people to the table for nourishment and conversation as I also kept a place for my burden.

My strife set a meal of trauma. Threat wove doubt and undoing into my food. Doubt flowed as the red dye over-filled my glass, staining bowls and disfiguring utensils. But I only knew how to not notice.

Recognizing wisdoms, talents and strengths in others—that I was sure I must deny myself—I argued for the seed of their humanity, a seed that must be nourished. Again and again, I offered and often demanded the nourishment of rain and sun... out there.

Whenever moss began to grow on my rock, whenever there was light for my space within, burden quickly filled the tiny orange and yellow blossoms that life's beauty sings. Trauma reminded me to scrape off the emerging growth and set it on other, truly deserving ground; this was the only option for me, the only viable option.

Defiant where I felt resistance, I persistently struggled where any possibility was only a memory. Laboring on when wind had carried my seeds away, I was left with the joy of knowing seeds without the rooted fineness of my full, petal-perfect conversation and sharing, without my sprouts and leaves receiving the nourishment of rain and the sun's warm embrace followed by the moon's soft caress under a star-filled sky.

Preaching Against labeling and dehumanizing, I rallied again and again, shouting Against inhumane boxes. I managed my campaign Against the expectations of "should," all the while proliferating the concept. Knowing the world was different, I needed people to rise up and show me that I was right—that humanity is not inhumane in its core.

It wasn't that I wanted to control people's lives—I wanted to change their conversations. Having changed my relationship with trauma, I was still strengthening my bond with it in ever more subtle ways.

I'm not unhappy with myself about these moments. I have danced with many beautiful people, inviting countless conversations to weave curiosity and inspiration as we glided across the dance floor. I have had the honor of being invited. I have marveled in each person I've encountered, including those few with whom I found no common interests.

Yet, I was also frustrated and angry and scared. And although I was so much more, although I wove beauty and wonder into conversations that held care while creativity and possibility brightened spaces as we shared amazing companionship, I was isolated.

Even when being held in the eyes and hearts of people who support and honor my creativity and possibility—those who have respected and supported my need to always find more—I still could not recognize the source of my frustration.

What was at the core of, "It has to better than this"? What did better mean for me, for my wellbeing and wholeness? I hadn't realized the possibility of choosing without threat; I didn't realize what I was arguing *for* as I continually clarified what I was Against.

How to choose without threat? How to freely partner with a life that grows from my heart as my heart opens in conversation with my breath and my breath flows in the continuous pulse of my unincumbered voice? How to simply be curious about the life I treasure, leaving battle on the battlefield with the fight?

How to choose without threat? How do we leave the battle on the battlefield?

I understand the frustration. I understand the fear that there isn't anything uncomplicated and substantive…that battles have to be won, lost or avoided.

A friend has gone inside to make us some breakfast. Let's go in and eat together. Let's share some stories and mingle our laughter over hot coffee and honeyed tea.

Please pass the oatmeal and a slice of cantaloupe. As for my story, I have come to realize that I can nourish the things I've always known to be true, growing myself beyond the burdens and the trauma, actually leaving these experiences in my past.

In his biography of fellow physicist Arthur Haas, Michael Wiescher noted:

> Haas' argument maintained that it is not nature that is complicated, it is only our way of making it understandable that is complicated. He presented these points of view with many examples from the microscopic world, a world

that, although it has always existed, has only today been made accessible and measurable by new means of observation.

—Michael Wiescher, in
Arthur E. Haas – The Hidden Pioneer of Quantum Mechanics

This passage excites me. I can see Haas reaching up to wipe off the fog that has accumulated on the inside of the windshield, making it possible to see a way forward.

If we allow ourselves, we are able to realize with "new means of observation." We are able to notice what is not complicated. We are able to choose, choosing to create from that which we are coming to realize.

> *If we allow ourselves, we are able to see with "new means of observation," to create from that which we are coming to realize.*

Let's begin with the breakfast we are eating, with what we choose for nourishment. Starting with basic understandings, we have learned that life's energy seems to be related to atoms and their activity. We have learned that this is the microscopic foundation for everything from the stars to our tastebuds.

With this clarity, we are able to trace various systems. We recognize the Sun and all that orbits in our solar system. We can also recognize that this very energy and its structure are what we hold in common.

We can recognize that we are of the same energy as the Earth that we live with and the squirrels scampering across the grass. That the trees and our children share an atomic identity that isn't as "complicated" as it is integral and "understandable."

When we aren't partnering with threat, we are no longer required to see differences. We are not required to mark variety as dissimilar. We can be curious about life's various structures and ways of participating.

New spaces open where we are able to invite new choices. New ways become available for our voices to speak. As our throats clear, new ways become available for how we will interact. We can live among differing ways of being present.

When we aren't partnering with threat, we are no longer required to see differences.

We can be curious about life's various structures and about ways of participating.

Very simply and practically, we can begin to realize how we're living. We can be curious about what our moments have in them. We can have wonder as we are fascinated with what we find.

Without inviting expectation, opinion, or judgement, we can, for example, talk about nourishing our bodies. I can notice as water softens my throat, hydration expanding my systems. I can notice how this oatmeal and peanut butter join with this juicy fruit, reaching both my tastebuds and my call for energy. I relax, breathing fully and easily thinking.

And, how we are eating may also enhance our capacity to threaten. We may have learned that we are safe in our ability to do battle, safe in our hard-won dominance and ability to exhibit control. So, we eat to prepare for this battle, consuming foods that cause imbalance and heighten the acid in our bodily systems. When we feel tired, stressed, overwhelmed, and frustrated, we might build ourselves up by preparing for threat, readying our bodies for conflict.

As though always needing to prepare for endurance, we consume considerable quantities of acid-forming carbohydrates and sugars, as well as fats. Even when the battle we are fighting is with threat itself, we nourish ourselves for the physical demand of combat. And our bodies respond accordingly: our blood pressure rises, we store fat, we prepare our bodies for the physical exertion that may never come.

Yet, our body's chemistry has been prepared for threat; our minds and senses stand alert, anticipating and then participating in some form of threat, even bullying ourselves about relaxing. Or, when we're exhausted by and can't escape from this prepared and anxious state that we began when our feet met the floor in the morning, we begin to coax ourselves to sleep with anything that will numb the threat so that we can arrive for the next day's endurance with enough stamina to survive the burden of being and feeling unsafe.

Even when we feel that we've accomplished something and wish to celebrate, we have learned to maintain our vigil. We feel safer, more relaxed, and even happy consuming an unbalancing quantity of acid-forming foods. As we learn to associate these foods with security from threat, we feel fortified as we celebrate—maintaining our readiness for battle.

While the list of symptoms that our bodies manifest from these choices is long and ranges from hair loss to organ failure, our choices for nourishment may continue to be determined by our relationship to threat. In response to these outcomes, we provide an entire medical community to support the insured. We create medications and various treatments to address the effects resulting from our relationship with trauma and anticipation of threat.

Through "normal" day-to-day experiences, we often embody additional, varying degrees of threat. As we circle the spectrum of trauma, breathing in threat and preparing for battle, our bodies navigate the world with us, meeting the burdens that arise from this relationship. While they can be as evident as the grave, these experiences result from our separation—separation from ourselves and our environment. We develop everything from allergies to tumors in the spaces that we leave vacant in our attempt to escape from threat and cope with trauma. Further, when we are involved in an accident,

> *We develop everything from allergies to tumors in the spaces that we leave vacant in our attempt to escape from threat.*

drastic weather event or similar experience, the familiar presence of threat defines and complicates our ability to restore and maintain balance and stability. Having established its place in our physical, cognitive and psychological components, trauma defines our body's crisis, automatically registering another threat to our wellbeing. Rather than re-establishing harmony and balance, we have learned to restore the apparent strength that we are convinced will keep trauma at bay and threat manageable.

For a large number of years, when my main objective was to avoid battle, I avoided food as well, reaching the point where my husband would bring food and sit to watch me eat.

When my stress and fear were at their highest, I avoided eating to keep my body "calm" and unpre-pared for participation, terrified that my rock would turn molten. In actuality, I was diving right in and decimating any precarious balance, exacerbating my body's sense of threat.

Struggle...Survive...Repeat...

At other times, when I had found people who seemed to know how to navigate threat with kindness and fun, I drank considerable amounts of iced coffee with can after can of cola, thrilling in the rush of preparedness, relishing what felt like the security of strength and invincibility.

All the while, I was engulfed in trauma.

My body's response to trauma heightened after my son was born. Terrified and convinced of my incapacity to provide safety for him, I hounded my doctor about my fragility. In frustration, she sent me for a spinal tap to prove that there was nothing wrong with me. Abnormal cell structure did, however, make evident that my relationship with trauma had indeed taken centerstage.

A few years later, I was the only patient to comment on the message taped to my gynecologist's mirror, "You are looking at the only person responsible for your health. Everyone else is just a consultant." And while relishing this shared truth, I continued to unconsciously consult with threat, trauma being my primary source for information. Abnormal cell growth on my cervix was followed by a lump in my breast.

Eventually I found a doctor in Chinatown who would rebalance the trauma lodged in my breast tissue with acupuncture and herbs. She wanted to see the x-ray so I went to retrieve my mammogram image. I was told that I couldn't have the film, that it belonged to the hospital.

Flabbergasted and outraged, I screamed to the man on the other side of the glass, asking if the hospital had been paid for the image. Consulting his computer, he nodded as the other people in the room turned to listen. I then asked if it was an image of my breast. He carefully nodded. I asked very loudly how, then, it could be that it wasn't my x-ray. I was given the film under very stern, non-negotiable terms; "my x-ray" was to be promptly returned.

Six months later, thermal imaging verified that my breast tissue was indeed healthy. Nonetheless, fibroid tumors in my uterus would bleed profusely into menopause, my body following the habit of bleeding that had begun just days after birth. I have intermittently used canes and wheelchairs to navigate through the red dye pulsing in my cells.

I was still surviving in a wash of trauma that brought the experience of threat to my body and my experience. Yet deep down, sitting on my rock and watching my frenetic dance, I knew what Haas had sought to prove: It is "not nature that is complicated, … [only my] way of making it understandable that is complicated."

When caring for ourselves—for our own individual components, including our bodies—in ways that match what we treasure, this is when we are not attempting to subdue or correct problems, problems that emerge from the "complicated" practice of nourishing what we don't want.

When we are caring for ourselves rather than tending to our relationship with trauma, we have an opportunity to hold ourselves and our planet in balance. As Jacque Nelson explained above, in these moments when we are "brave enough to not be brave," we can allow "ourselves to innately understand that sometimes not being brave is the bravest thing we ever do."

> When we are caring for ourselves rather than tending to our relationship with trauma, we have an opportunity to hold ourselves and our planet in balance.

In these moments, threat is out on the porch. Trauma is not seated at our table.

In these moments, we can touch what we do want. Our senses bring us information. We are able to base our lives on the treasures we are, bringing joy. With practice we learn to notice what feels natural and uncomplicated, what nurtures and nourishes who we know ourselves to be.

FINDING A WAY TO CHOOSING

These words come from a place within me. Waves of thought and memory flow through my life's experience, giving trauma to itself and leaving threat where it lives. I am finding and creating a new spectrum. This wave of light matches my growing passions and connections as I move forward.

Honoring my feelings and choosing what feels breathful, I am learning to recognize the "should-s" when they pop up and I continue to appreciate my expanding realizations. The relief of, "I choose this way" brings kindness and generosity. Grace moves with security and thriving. I've begun to realize that my joy is possible.

Finding and dancing with what nourishes me, my true self has cracked open. My green succulent sprouts are strengthening, just like the sprouts that I anticipate with such delight in springtime. I recognize my uncomplicated part in life. Some of my sprouts are forming branches, like this book, while others are just beginning to emerge, wiggling in the mud.

As we sit on the grass and watch the sun fill the horizon, I realize that my life changes when I spend more time with and for myself.

Now I pause when I hear my inner bully speaking; I have come to realize that nearly every thought I was having was in response to the threat in my head, which always had a comment.

These reminders saved my life at one time. They helped me to avoid the physical and emotional attacks that kept my family moving in the direction they were traveling. I had gratefully taken my own bully's directives. These guidelines were the only light in a dark tunnel; the only thing I had found to be safely Against was myself.

I'm grateful that I didn't expand much further in my threat to myself. Beyond attempted suicides when I was sure that "better" just didn't come anywhere close to "good," I didn't take measures to escape. Apart from those weeks when my son moved to his big-boy bed, I didn't turn to alcohol.

I was terrified much of the time, not feeling strong enough to face the threat that I saw at every turn. But at just those moments of consuming despair, a friend would step in and take the other hand, the hand not clenched around oozing hopeless threat.

In fifth grade, besides the grass and the cat, there was my teacher who went for Saturday walks with me; I taught her how to ice skate. Years later, when I carefully explained to another friend that I didn't have what it took to be her friend, she said we'd just find a way together.

In college, my student teacher had cement blocks in his yard and he let me hurl them from far above my head as I wailed into the trees around me. After my psychiatrist told me I'd never be able to stop taking the medications that made me so sick and disoriented— "People with your history will always need extra support." —I heard the doorbell ringing; two people had already pounded on the windows without my hearing but I answered this third attempt. My friend asked what the hell I was doing, noting the trail of blood that was dripping from my punctured veins.

Years later, a friend happened to phone on the day I was through with life's burden, saying that she heard something new in my voice and she'd be there in an hour.

I wrote a letter to my gynecologist explaining that I wouldn't be able to see him any longer. He invited me to his office, saying that he needed me to explain. After hearing what I had to say (my mother was also his patient and as my life changed, I needed to be sure that I wouldn't accidentally meet her), he offered a possible way forward that I was grateful to accept.

And during the last quarterly visit to my neurologist, when he announced his retirement, he explained that while he had been monitoring my health, finding a new neurologist would only be a "maintenance move." As we said our goodbyes, he asked me not to cry because he had other patients to see and couldn't be that sad just then.

On a very long and dreary afternoon, an agency sent a woman who sat at my kitchen table after cleaning the dishes and my bathroom. She asked why I was here. She stated that if she had to live my life, she'd just kill herself. She reminded me of the nurse in the maternity ward who had snarled at me in disgust. She had assured me that I would be a horrible mother—as I sat there struggling to breathe despite the liquid in my lungs, holding my son who was not able to nurse.

My momentum and stamina to be Against myself and the ways of the world grew alongside my attempts to stretch and grow in my own skin. In the process, I became intimate with the "one step forward, two steps back" approach.

It was many years before I understood that being Against something was inviting that very thing. That being Against something meant I was inviting it to dinner and then taking it dancing. While standing Against, I was continuing to build my ever-more-intimate relationship with threat and thereby trauma. As we noted earlier, it's interesting to notice that while I don't need to capitalize "threat" or "trauma," which stand out in our minds as what they are, we are so conditioned to be Against that the meaning is missed if I simply write "against."

This is how tightly Against is woven through the spectrum of our lives. Grasping for safety and survival, we have tangled Against around our senses.

When threat is partnered with Against, everything is saturated with red dye that seeps into and fills the very fibers of our senses. Red dye overrides our ability to see, hear, taste, smell and touch the world. Our senses are meant to give us information so that we can easily make choices on our own behalf. Yet, these senses have become clogged with perceptions that are so involved with trauma that they no longer move with us. For, although our senses are a part of who we actually are, they are no longer purely informing us about ourselves or anything else.

Although our senses are a part of who we actually are, they are no longer purely informing us about ourselves or anything else.

With our clear senses, we can taste the richness of life—the scent of morning waking and stretching with us, celebrating life even on the way to the bathroom. Our sixth sense, the combination of our senses, is also a part of every moment. Although often deemed silly and unprovable, this is what keeps us alive and finding our way, even when unacknowledged and taken for granted.

Uncomplicated atoms remain components of all that we experience. Uncomplicated atoms that are common to everything, including our planet. Yet, we have become threatened by the planet itself, by ourselves, by each other, by life … as we threaten right back.

I began with admitting that there was a bully in my head. Next was hearing—actually, lovingly listening to her. Soon, I became curious about the barrage of Against messages that I was inundating myself with. Sometimes being Against Against, I would be running on a pretty small hamster wheel.

Committed to finding my way forward, I realized that I could follow the thread of any particular bullying; this bullying was inevitably tied to my tangle of threat and wrapped in trauma of some sort. For example, "What's wrong with you? You know you can't afford that!" was part of a thread that led to feeling inadequate while wanting to feel that I could do something interesting, which became tangled with the threat of lack and not having enough, which was tied to feeling that I'd missed a passionate and meaningful life, missed work that would bring funds for enjoyment and fruitful engagement, proving that I was undeserving, inept and couldn't get it right.

Hearing myself and my belief that the world was for me impenetrable, I became aware that I was not nourishing my ability to act on my own behalf. I was circling in my experiences of trauma and the threat I had grown comfortable with, unhappy and comfortable. This brought the question, "What can I do to change this?"

Questions that follow a realization can open doors, creating options in a different voice: "This feels awful. What can I do that feels more like me?" With curiosity, wondering brings questions that suggest opportunities. Opportunities emerge that match our treasures as we begin to see more clearly.

> *With curiosity, wondering brings questions that suggest opportunities.*

Red dye is no longer filtering out possibilities. When I can see with curiosity, stepping stones are visible as my spaces clear within me. This allows me to see, hear, and even taste a new opportunity, touch a new way.

These openings come in batches. Atoms are all linked together, making up who I am. So, as I make my way through one tangle, others unravel. As I follow a thread to its knot around some precious aspect of myself, untying that knot frees a part of me to move and grow so that other knots simply untangle, perhaps without even being noticed. Until one day, I simply and naturally do something that I never dreamed I would or could, something that is filled with my passion.

Something true of me moves. A treasure, free from the barrage of Against, announces a moment. For me, this is living from my rock.

Many years ago, in that time when I was sitting on the floor with my therapist, she had guided me to a support group for survivors of sexual abuse. On the night of our first meeting, I was pretty confused as I looked around the circle. I have since learned that people feel empowered by the term "survivor," feeling bolstered up when saying that they have survived a traumatizing experience. That night, I was having a different experience.

Frustrated, I asked if there were people who had made it past this point. It seemed obvious that we'd survived; if we hadn't survived, we wouldn't be sitting in the circle. There we were, about ten of us, and the reality that we had survived didn't feel like much of an accomplishment to me. So I asked, "What about these others, those we can be like when we "heal"? Why aren't they here to tell us what it's like after this?"

It's only now that I realize, they're all—We're All—still fundamentally surviving. Today in a grocery store, people were gunned down by a man with a rifle. Last week a group of people in a day spa were massacred while still further from here, governments are again creating mass graves for their citizens. Our connected collective atoms are simply and effortlessly killing each other like a cancer, white sheets no longer needed for murders that occur in plain view.

Being "healed" isn't working when the optimal goal is surviving.

During a philosophy class, the professor asked us to raise a hand if we had ever felt like an alien, like we weren't meant to be here. Every person in the room put up a hand.

We as humanity will not feel included—part of the whole of life—as long as we are alienated from ourselves, from our treasures. While we live as though our treasures are part of a non-congruent life force, we will continue to treat others as though they don't belong either.

> We as humanity will not feel included— as long as we are alienated from ourselves.

Threat will continue to lurk as we feel alienated and are therefore alienating others. Change involves new choices, not from the "top" or the "bottom"—from ourselves, right where we are.

> Threat will continue to lurk as we feel alienated and are therefore alienating others.

Each moment of each day is an opportunity to practice being me. With this focus, ambition and desire, my non-alien life occurs. I can actually choose if Against is invited to address a recognized threat and add to my string of traumas. I won't recognize the choice each time, in the moment. At first, probably most often only in retrospect. And, I will still be choosing. I will be practicing being me. Discovering what I have to offer. Will I practice being me in this moment? What does that look like today? Will I invite Against to bring threat for a collaboration?

Yesterday my phone rang. Someone very dear to me said that there was a bomb squad in his parking lot near the trash bin. We talked together for an hour while robots patrolled the area around the apartment building. Apparently no more homemade explosives were found. The people in black windbreakers left with their trailer of detection equipment.

Obviously disturbed, we were relieved when nothing exploded. Now we knew that this was a possible scenario, one that we had never considered in our personal experience. And—I was delighted as I realized that I hadn't chosen to be Against the crisis.

I didn't use the opportunity to add to my or our trauma. I practiced being myself: hearing all of the ways that the situation was impacting our conversation and realizing the elements of what was happening (i.e., they weren't evacuating the building or doing a door-to-door search). With complete attention and care, I felt calm and very relieved when all was well and we ended our call.

I wasn't exhausted, overwhelmed, or afraid. I simply shifted to the next thing. I'm so incredibly grateful to be able to choose—to live from my rock, reaching among my treasures for balancing.

Yet, I know full well that crisis is "out there," regardless of where I am. And with it, the possibility that I will shift to surviving. How then will I be able to continue when there is risk to my life, my honor, my care, my ability to be embraced and to embrace? How else, if not with love?

I nod and then I stop, sit back and take a long slow breath. Are there different ways to love? Does love come in different seasons and shapes like the flowers in the garden?

I have noticed that when an ideal, an external "truth" is the only thing to trust—when faith in love, for example, is set out like a signal flare to guide us as we continue on the battlefield—then we remain lost on that "hallowed ground." Whether on a field in Gettysburg, Pennsylvania or the site of two towers in New York City, whether a church in Alabama or a grocery store in the Rocky Mountains, whether

> *I have noticed that when an ideal, an external "truth" is the only thing to trust—when faith in love, for example, is set out like a signal flare to guide us as we continue on the battlefield—then we remain lost.*

pavement in Minnesota or a sandy beach in Indiana, when love isn't carried from personal wellbeing — burning bright from the treasures within — we can follow that torch but we will still be on the battle-field. We will trip over corpses and eventually drown in the trauma.

So how do we take this vision and travel? How do we span the distance from "what has been" to a place where "new opportunities are happening"? Where will we be connected and present?

Where can we each realize the relief of balance? When we often know love as a survival tactic, how do we join together and thrive? How do we tend the mud to grow the seeds that are living beneath such arid ground?

I think we are able to make life simpler still. I don't think it's actually complicated. We can put our feet in the soil around our rocks. We can look to see what is growing in our pulsing mud, there where we've stopped being brave, stopped searching for the way through. From our rocks, we can touch that place where our seeds are ready to sprout. Sprouts that are relying exclusively on our attention in order to flourish.

FIRST WITH OURSELVES

People have said that I am an exception, that finding options and a wonderful life are not possible for everyone, that for some the battle is the only way.

Each one, every one of us, you and I can, in the space between the inhale and the exhale, each of us can feel the relief of, "I truly am enough." We can choose to stop being brave for a little bit, and then a little more.

I truly am enough.

I know this because I've been watching. I know this because I've been living. I've seen us fighting to survive because we are fighting to protect.

Yet, nothing that is organic—that lives and blooms with water and is fed by care—has ever thrived when tended by hands that hold hot lava, molten ash flowing to traumatize every cell, hands that rise to our faces, limiting our ability to see anything beyond inevitable demise...*survive, rinse, repeat.*

I don't have a silver bullet.

I do know that each of us is an amazing human capacity.

Each of us can be "brave enough to not be brave" for a moment.

In that moment we can hear our own hearts beating and over a string of moments, we can each follow our unique pulse until we find our curiosity. I know that we can each remember how to wonder, how to be curious. We can stand or sit or lie on the earth and feel that we are home. We can read a book to a child or giggle as the wind jumps with a grasshopper or look into the eyes we find in the mirror. And I know these moments feed our humanity.

How do we reach through unsustainable survival and into the immediacy of ourselves? How can we address the power of an assault, of a rifle? I too have wondered how our personal wisdom, honoring, and care will reach through the fires that seem to engulf us.

As we attempt to control the threat, as we wail—in waves of traumatized anguish and loss—for laws that will control brutality and the influx of weapons, we can take a breath and pause. For just a moment, for a single beat of our wounded hearts, we can realize that the crisis won't be truly addressed with counter threats. A larger fist raised in defiance won't be a bigger threat to those whose very breath is threatened by the thought of losing their only weapon Against the onslaught to *their* identities.

These wounds won't be healed.

I once thought that accountability would open the doors and free the people. I thought that a world where Nelson Mandela's Truth and Reconciliation Commission had existed also held hope and vision that would shine in its simple warmth, opening possibility.

Looking more closely, I recognize the possibility of connections. I notice presence, hearts leaning into the moment, no longer holding onto threat. Where crisis is admitted without threat, a commitment to honesty and self-

> *Where crisis is admitted without threat, a commitment to honesty and self-realization can bring relief and nourishment.*

realization can bring relief and nourishment. There could be room at the table then, room for the possibility of each person reaching out and joining each other person.

Opportunity born of conversation, conversation slowed not for accountability but for something else—the human capacity of connection. Connection carried not by another bullet or the tightening of another rope, not by laws. Rather, voices can speak, emerging from within those seated at the table.

Violence and war, assault and trauma, which exist only because we carry them gingerly forward in our steps, have not been controlled so far. Why do we persist with this lack of achievement? The war to be right and win out has not been won. We have not accomplished security, a place in this field of rightness. We still don't come close to winning. What is our thinking? Why do we think faster bullets, still more-discreet bombs, rules, laws and statutes will win?

Is it time to try another way? There are other options.

When I wake up in the morning to be right or when, after lunch, I find that I need to be right so that

I feel safe—from the influx of anguished phone calls, the texts of turmoil, the newsfeeds bringing threat to wrap around my ankles—then I go to bed at night with my mind racing, listening to the sirens wailing across the river.

When I wake up bringing a smile across my back, anticipating the morning sky, my eyes lighting as the sun warms the day, I find that I feel the winds blowing softly past, my leaves rustling with care and curiosity when the phone rings. And when later I remember to pause and take a full breath, the text messages again buzz along as I work at my tasks. At night, I can find my relax, shifting into sleep.

Admitting that I often choose the first, I commit to practicing my reach for the latter, offering myself moments of living—with me—into the world.

If not in that moment, then with this breath.

Choosing to struggle—calling in threat—drowning in trauma—is an inside job. What will I choose?

Choosing to be present, to connect with our-selves. Finding trails that are not trials, paths with signposts designating relief and sustenance, curving to loosen tangles and ease our way forward. The

> *The simplicity of thriving won't be found on the path of resistance, nor on the path of least resistance.*

simplicity of thriving won't be found on the path of resistance, nor on the path of least resistance. Our individual paths follow bridges of realizing and involve practicing the warmth of self, opening curiosity with the next breath.

Will we blow a bit of our breath into our own soil?

Right here, at the base of our experiencing, will we clear the red dye from our eyes to see what's growing from our seeds?

> *Will we blow a bit of our breath into our own soil?*

Sprouts emerge. As they are tended, these sprouts will flourish with and for you...in the growing and emerging space vacated by trauma. Threat won't have the same hold over the next breath ... now two ... now three ...

There's Either and Or ... and now, a third option.

For me, I looked around and felt my space. I was curious about what my rock would be like when it wasn't on top of and holding in all of those experiences. Slowly the wonder of sitting on my rock changed to curiosity and I came to notice that I wasn't actually sitting on a rock that was isolated.

I sit on a rock surrounded by trees that all have spaces for me. My spaces hold what I love. My treasures sit in the bark, climb the branches, sprout and flutter with the leaves, sail in scarlet and orange wonder to be tickled by the grass as autumn's light shits. Crevices share stories with snow, some provide wood for a fire where a gathering of conversation drifts into sunrise.

Seeds are sprouting. Roots reaching into the earth will nourish this new table. A new spectrum is coming into focus as my leaves breathe in exchange with atmosphere, creating rainbows whose ends touch pots brimming with connection, presence, ease, harmony and yes, love. And each day I choose less threat. I am engulfed less often in less trauma… and, truly, less is more—and I am me.

I've heard that it seems an insurmountable task, learning how to choose. Like even more struggle, this clarifying and choosing. I've felt and seen threat's bully override change, possibility judged as only available to "the few," if any.

There's a lesson, the question being, "Which monster will you feed?" … How can I be happy when I know there are monsters? When I know where they live, have anticipated their arrival? When I see clearly how they could just keep coming?

I'm happy when I remember that I am not a monster. In this moment, I am not a monster. In this moment, I have that choice.

I'm nourished and well-fed when I put my plate in front of me at the table, feeding what I value, hold dear, choose to grow. I don't often have

In this moment,
I am not a monster.
In this moment,
I have that choice.

secret signs etched on my door saying, "Trauma lives here," letting monsters know that they can enter through the window or the door around back. Nor do I usually have "Do Not Enter" signs plastered on the walls with yellow police tape wrapped around the perimeter. There is simply no such invitation being initiated, by either discussion or resistance.

When I no longer choose between monsters, I choose me. I choose gently running my fingers along a honeysuckle's throat as she bounces on her free-roaming vine in evening's pause. I find that life feeds me and I feel what I love. I'm happy when I nod at your belief in monsters while seeing the shimmering flowers that you're growing, tending or hiding for another time.

> *When I no longer choose between monsters, I choose me.*

Grief and loss wash through me as the tide, experiences felt and flowing with the next realizations. I am receiving that perfect bite of nourishment, nourishment that feeds the very wiggle of me. Nourishment with enough food for the seeds that flow out of me to exchange with another garden, with lives that match the joy found here in me.

My "Welcome" mat to the door of me is a path bordered in bright purples and pinks swaying with yellows and oranges along the walkway. My pulse is wide and smiling when I see you coming and I'm curious about what you enjoy and what you will offer that moves in synch with me, that offers a harmony and perhaps a differing rhythm that I hadn't imagined.

I don't know what your seeds hold in your place deep inside, in that place where your amazing and wondrous human capacity—your rock—is alive and well. I just know they're there, both your space and your human capacity continually germinating possibilities. And I know you can find it all.

If you reach into the pocket of your sweater or coat, there's a bottle of bubbles there. Let's set the bottles with their wands on the soil together with the treasures we've been holding, side by side...

... Let's open each
noticing our breath, as our inhale follows our exhale
Let's take up the wand between our wet fingers
feeling the circle filled with shimmering
Let's part our lips a bit and feel our breath blow
iridescent newly born opportunity
Let's create a spectrum of growth
born in the hush of hearing
flowing from choice
Let's join the table with ease
where tastes are nourishing
brave spaces within ...

GLOSSARY OF CONCEPTS

Against: A response of choosing to be in opposition, closing off alternatives and possibilities by tightening parameters.

And: Life as an evolving opportunity.

Based on: What we base our choices on; what we listen to as our source(s) for information.

Brave: When a desired way forward is unclear, summoning our grit and being present on our own behalf. From the perspective of trauma, being brave can be about pushing on regardless of how we are feeling.

Burden: Experience that is difficult to carry around. Sometimes these are experiences that we don't allow to develop as we shift and change, so they become heavy and obstructive. At other times these experiences can actually be a part of someone else's story and have become heavy because they are no longer ours to move with.

Choice(s), (n): Opportunity; how we can be present, how we can participate in a particular moment. With choice, we are also able to participate or perhaps not participate with an occurrence, in a moment.

Choosing: Opening to an experience. We may open knowingly, through habit, or—for various reasons—

without considering our choices. We can, for example, open to the experience of welcoming, to the experience of declining, or to the experience of closing off.

Conversation: A multifaceted, honoring exchange. An opportunity to speak from within who we are and what we have to offer, while hearing ourselves speaking, and to listen, activating our ability to hear what another is saying.

Curiosity: Open wonder. Engaging our senses for discovery. Curiosity is always with us and available, making thriving possible and supporting us during crisis and grief so that we can remain connected with ourselves and able to recognize our choices.

Curious: Inviting exchange in the moment. When we are curious, we are able to open with wonder and to recognize varying occurrences and choices.

Either/Or: Categories that mold life, ourselves and our experiences as predetermined, stagnant concepts.

Experience: An opportunity to exercise who we are or are choosing to be, with the choices we make. With threat, experience often becomes something that is happening to us rather than being something we are a part of creating.

Grace: Honoring our true selves and thereby honoring others and all of life, while honoring all of life, including ourselves, others and our ways.

Hiding: A layering of perception that is brought into practice when we feel threatened. Hiding often involves placing layers of previous experience between who we are and what is occurring, so that we are not seen or perceived (by ourselves or another) — as we truly are —in the moment.

Justification: Evidence that is presented to validate the choices we have made, are intending to make, and that we maintain as necessary. The need to justify is part of the practice of threat.

Limited: Within parameters. When we are afraid of being overwhelmed, we may construct a limited environment as a way of attempting to control what happens. This is significantly different from, for example, reaching one's limit as a signal to move on or change direction; these choices keep us engaged so that we are naturally free and not overwhelmed.

Opinion: An idea or belief based on something outside of oneself. For example, when we choose based on who we are, we are expressing ourselves within the whole of humanity. Whereas with an opinion, we are setting ourselves apart.

Opportunity: A moment of choosing.

Participate: To take part in, consciously or unconsciously, and thereby to contribute to its existence.

Perpetrate: To act upon without conscious, informed consent.

Possibility: Opportunity to be curious, create, choose, love. Also, creating, choosing, loving and being curious are moving with possibility.

Predetermined: Engaging based on information from our previous experience or/and from the experience of others and then basing our choices on this prior experience, thereby altering our perceptions about what is currently occurring in the moment.

Rhythm: A pulse. The pulse of our own hearts, of a moment, an experience, an interaction or exchange; part of how the moment is perceived.

(My) Rock: A surety. Knowing and trusting of self; a place within us where we know who we are; a place that is always present with and accessible to us, part of the treasure we are. It simply is, cannot be proven and so does not need to be protected. Interacting with our rocks is, however, a choice.

Should(ing): A predetermined expectation that has arrived from outside of ourselves; a judgement that we may have incorporated as our own.

Side by side: Experiences set next to each other. We can look to see how these experiences may be interwoven, how they might be moving together and informing each other. When we recognize the arrangement, we can recognize how these experiences are affecting each other; we can choose what we want to continue to partner with and what to let move on from the relationship. When we put our palms out in front of us and then place our hands next to each other, we can recognize the coming together of experiences; in separating our hands, we can see that both experiences exist simultaneously without needing to be joined.

Sorting: Separating one from another, either as groups or as individuals, based on opinion or judgement. We also sort by experience and based on our expectation.

Suffering: A painful exchange that we can simply move through or maintain in our held experience, thereby adding to the experience of burden and trauma.

Third option: Those ideas, inventions, experiences, and invitations that emerge beyond the known, the already imagined, or the experienced. The third option is a new opportunity, an opening.

Threat: The perception, belief, or understanding that our wellbeing is at risk.

Thriving: Being engaged with our selves, our treasures in fluid exchange of giving and receiving with all of life.

Trauma: Living with the experience of threat.

Treasures: Our aspects, those pure elements of who we are before any other experience has informed us about ourselves. We can learn about, interact with, and expand our treasures with experience yet, with or without these opportunities, our treasures make up who we are.

True care: Care for ourselves and each other that naturally radiates as an interactive presence, as we live from our wellbeing.

Victim: A belief that we are not well, that our wellbeing is dependent on something or someone outside of ourselves.

Wellbeing: Who we are, individually and collectively, as part of life itself. We can know and experience our wellbeing. Wellbeing can never be eliminated; we can, however, not recognize its presence.

Further Reading

Kathleen Aharoni, Ann Boyd, *I breathe my own breath* (Milwaukee: HenschelHAUS, 2017)

Eldad Arad, Libby Mislan, *The Shaya I Know* (self-published, 2021).

Shel Silverstein, *A Giraffe and a Half* (New York: HarperCollins, 1964).

ABOUT THE AUTHOR

Curious and ready to explore, Elizabeth taught herself to read by the age of three. She soon moved from her little red rocker to the tree outside, reading to the neighborhood's stray cat. She was ready for new horizons when school began. From tutoring to basketball, drama and the school newspaper, Elizabeth was off gathering information from the worlds she explored.

Elizabeth maintained an intimate relationship with nature, as she grew up in the midst of Watergate and the Vietnam war. She became convinced, in her teens, that we are in need of a "paradigm shift."

With BA degrees in both English literature and philosophy, Elizabeth sees how the very nature of our thoughts is woven with aspects of survival and threat. Yet, Elizabeth didn't commit herself to academia or the struggles of humanity. Persistent in her passion to see and understand, conversation remains at the center of her world.

When climate change and the pandemic of 2020 began shifting our paradigms, Elizabeth expanded her writing to include books that open further conversation.

You are invited to join in this conversation
and to visit
www.ChoosingNewWaysForward.com